ZEN
AND NOTES FOR NOTHING

FURTHER ZEN RAMBLINGS FROM THE INTERNET

SCOTT SHAW

BUDDHA ROSE PUBLICATIONS

Zen and Notes for Nothing
Copyright © 2023 by Scott Shaw
www.scottshaw.com
ALL RIGHTS RESERVED

Cover Photograph by Scott Shaw
Copyright © 2023—All Rights Reserved

Rear Cover Photograph of Scott Shaw
by Hae Won Shin
Copyright © 2023—All Rights Reserved

First Edition 2023

This book contains material protected under International and Federal Copyright Laws and Treaties. Any unauthorized reprint or use of this material is prohibited. No part of this book may be reproduced or transmitted in any form or by any means, electronic or mechanical, including photocopying, recording, or by any information storage and retrieval system without express written permission from the author or publisher.

ISBN 10: 1-949251-50-0
ISBN 13: 978-1-949251-50-0

Library of Congress Control Number: 2023931065

10 9 8 7 6 5 4 3 2 1
Printed in the United States of America

Zen and Notes for Nothing

Introduction

Here it is, *The Scott Shaw Zen Blog 25.0,* originally presented on the *World Wide Web.* All of the writings presented in this book were written between September of 2022 and January of 2023.

As was the case with the previously published volumes based upon *The Scott Shaw Zen Blog;* entitled: *Scribbles on the Restroom Wall, The Chronicles: Zen Ramblings from the Internet, Words in the Wind, Zen Mind Life Thoughts, The Zen of Life, Lies and Aberrant Reality, Apostrophe Zen, The Abstract Arsenal of Zen and the Psychology of Being, Zen and Again: The Metaphysical Philosophy of Psychology, Tempest in a Teapot and the Den of Zen, Buddha in the Looking Glass, Wo Ton' of the Blue Vision, Zen and the Psychology of the Spiritual Something, Pyrophoric Zen, Fragments of Paradox, Zen: Traversing the Entity of Non-Entity, Zen and the Ambient Echo: The Psychological Philosophy of Being, Paritical Zen and the Life Science of Becoming No Thing, Obscurist Occulto: Hiding from the Definition of Meaning, Principles of the Precepts, Left Turn at Reality Central, Zen and the Outside of the Inside, Garage Sale Zen,* and *The Zen of Volume Destiny* this volume is presented exactly as it was viewed on *scottshaw.com* with no rewriting, punctuation, or typo corrections. From this, we hope you will receive the original reading experience.

This volume of internet ramblings is presented with the date and time listed as to when each blog was originally posted. Also, the blogs in this volume are presented from last to first. With this, we hope to present a transcendence back through time as opposed to an evolving evolution. In addition, we left out the traditional *Table of Contents* in an attempt to leave this volume with a much more free-flowing reading experience.

Okay, there's the information and the definitions. Read on... We hope you enjoy it. And, be sure to stayed tuned for the ongoing *Scott Shaw Zen Blog* @ *scottshaw.com*.

Alpha and Beta
11/Jan/2023 08:29 AM

In all relationships, between two people, there is the alpha and there is the beta. There is the person who is the driving force and there is the one who is more submissive. Of course, the varying levels of this equation are vast, but if you look to any interpersonal association you can quickly view which element each individual inhabits.

This defining factor has caused many relationships to succeed, and it has caused many to fail. The failure usually comes about when the individual who is on the beta side decides that they no longer wish to hold that position.

This being stated, take a moment right now and look to your own relationships. Who is the alpha and who is the beta in each of them? Once you have defined this, pick one of your personal connections out in particular and truly peer into the complexities of that joining.

Are you happy and are you okay with the way this yin and yang works? If you are, why are you? If you are not, why aren't you? And, perhaps more importantly, if you are not, why do you maintain the relationship in its current status?

The answer to this question for many, and the reason why most people are willing to inhabit the beta position in some, if not all of their relationships is that, it provides them with that Some-Thing that they need or want. But, the question that then must be truly explored is, what is the cost of that relationship to your life and to your karma?

I imagine that most of us, as we have passed through our life, have allowed someone to cause us to do something that we did not really feel right about. Hopefully, that not-right-ness was something very small and it did not hurt the overall development of your life, or perhaps more importantly, it did not hurt someone else. If it did hurt your life, if what you were directed to do did hurt someone else, how did that affect your relationship with the alpha-factor? And, more importantly, what did you do to correct, redo, or undo what you were caused to do?

Really think about this because it is an important life factor that you should sincerely consider.

If you watch closely, sometimes you can see when two people are interacting that one of them would like to state their opinion, which is different from the person who is predominately speaking, change the direction of the conversation, or maybe even guide the discussion in a different direction, but to the overpowering nature of the alpha, they cannot. Here lies one of the primary problems in the alpha/beta relationship. It is not uncommon that the alpha dominates and leaves little room for the true personality, ideas, or ideology of the beta individual to be revealed.

One of the ultimate truths of existence is that everyone's life is predominately based upon the choices they make. This being understood, are you the driving factor in the choices you make? Or, do you allow someone else to guide you and your choices towards things that you may not feel are right at the depths of your being? If so, what choice are you going to make about this understanding?

If we look at life-relationships, if we watch the speech and the reactions of two people who are in a relationship, (however that relationship may be defined), we can quickly see when one element of that association differs from what the other one is saying or doing in any given moment of time. Just look, just see, just observe. But, once this is observed, though we can witness it, we may even be able to call it out, it is only for those two people to decide if what the other one is doing is actually acceptable to the person on the beta side of the equation.

In life, you have a choice to make. You can be friends, lovers, life-partners, business associates, or whatever, but in doing that, if you allow the alpha-factor to drive your words, actions, and your life-deeds, what have you actually contributed to the great good of the overall all? What have you stood for and stood up for in your own life definition? How have shaped the direction of the conversation and what comes out of any interaction the two of you have had?

Your life is your choice. Will you allow the alpha to guide all that you accomplish, or will you take the reins and guide your own life direction? Your Life. You Choice. Are you alpha or are you beta?

* * *
11/Jan/2023 07:26 AM

If you create negative events with your words or with your actions, that negativity spreads outwards forever.

If you create positive events with your words or with your actions, that positivity spreads outwards forever.

What do you want to be responsible for unleashing?

You Have to Know Yourself to Forget Yourself
10/Jan/2023 01:57 PM

In Zen, the practitioner consciously focuses on the loss of Self, known as Śūnyatā. From Sanskrit, Śūnyatā means, *"Emptiness."* This is one of the cornerstone techniques of Zen Buddhism. In the Theravāda tradition of Buddhism, Śūnyatā is commonly understood to mean, *"No-Self."* Though this is an idealized sought-after goal of Buddhism, think about how many people live in a void of consciousness that is absent from any conscious reality. Does that mean that they are living the spiritual existence of No-Self?

Look around the world, how many people are conscious of their actions verses how many people simply act and react? How about you? Are your actions and reactions done with a sense of dedicate purpose or are they just an undefined response?

You see, this is where a life lived consciously, with a focused purpose, comes in direct opposition to those who live their life with a lack of internal definition. Yes, many people set goals for themselves and set about on a path to obtaining them. From this, they claim they possess a purpose. But, as a worldly goal is as temporal as obtaining that object or that something, is that a pathway to salvation?

Think about a goal you once had about obtaining that Something. What were you willing to do to get it? What did you do to get it? What did getting it cost you? And, what did you getting it cost others? Then, if you did get it, what happened to you after you got it? Were all of your need(s) forever met? Or, once you got it, did you once again place a new goal on your life road for you to chase after?

This is the same for those who seek after a certain person. Think about all of the people who have placed their focus on bringing a specific someone into their life. Think about all of the things they did to get them. We have all heard stories about those who have done some really crazy things to get that someone into a relationships. But, how many of those relationships last? How many of them end in disaster and pain? And, how much hurt was created and amplified in the process? Is that a pathway to life salvation?

How about you? Think of the roads you have walked in the obtaining of your desires, goals, and relationships. What have they meant to the overall evolution your life? Was the pathway to you getting them and the living of you living of them, (if you actually did get to live them), the answer to all of your needs? Or, did they simply lead to your desiring something more based upon what you (now) already possessed?

What about the other person? What about that person you desired and you possibly brought into your life? What did that coupling mean to their life? Was it more or was it less to them compared to what it was to you? What was the ultimate outcome? Did it make their life better? And, what consequences emulated from you two coming together to the life of others and the greater world as a whole? Did it provide spiritual awakening?

Again, we come back to doing verses non-doing. Those who have a so-called, *"Purpose,"* verses those who do not. We come back to the ultimate outcome of your doing based in your desire and your wanting. What does any of it truly equal? This is the question that few people ponder. They just WANT.

If we look into this subject a bit deeper, have you ever met a pathological liar? Someone who lies about everything. I'm sure we have all had a lie or two told to us throughout our lifetime. I imagine you have told a lie or two. But, for some, they just lie. Even if you bring this to their attention, even if you ask them to stop, even if you tell them it is damaging your relationship, they continue. Why is this?

The thing is, one could argue that an individual who holds this mindset is embracing a space of No-Self because what they have envisioned in their mind holds no correlation with reality. Thus, as it means nothing, it is nothing. They may tell someone a lie about themselves (or whatever) and that other person may believe them, thereby making that lie a truth. At least a truth in the mind of the person who was lied to. But, if what anyone speaks or believes is based in a fabrication of reality, where is the essence of anything? All is just lost to the realms of fabrication. Is that spiritual nothingness?

Another example is, have you ever met a person that is so into their job that even when they are not doing it, they are thinking about it? This mindset can transition to all kinds of different levels, be it playing a musical instrument, dancing, doing the marital arts, surfing, running, whatever... Even when they are not doing it, they are thinking about doing it or are playing scenarios about the subject out in their mind. This is intense focus. Does that make them better at whatever it is they are constantly thinking about? Probably. But, does that give them universal knowledge and expansive inner-truth? No, not really. It just provides them with the drug of distraction.

All things physical are only physical and they pass away with time. The body gets old, companies go out of business, and then what is a person who focuses their life with this intensity left with? Nothing. A life live for something outside of themselves that eventually will be gone.

Think about a religion that you do not practice. For most, when they hear about the beliefs of others, they simply dismiss them as hogwash. They think, *"How can anyone believe that nonsense."* Now, think about your own religion, how many people think that about what you believe? Yet, does that change your system of belief? Probably not.

But, is believing the basis of truth or is believing simply a method for an individual to live in a state of denial?

You see, in all of the religions, (which is the defining factor of so many people's life), there is no ONE absolute truth. There is only the belief that is held in the mind of each person. What this tells is that all the Mind Stuff out there, all the beliefs, all the desires, (even the desire for enlightenment), is nothing more than a projection of something to keep one thinking and on the road to obtaining, which is in direct contrast to Śūnyatā.

Even people who claim to hold some sort of extra-religious knowledge or know and teach some supposed religious truth; are they living the truth or are they just living a lie that is solely projected from their own mind? From my experience, some of which I have detained in this blog over the years, most of those who claim spirituality are the farthest thing from it. Meaning, claimed spirituality is not the definition of spirituality. Just because you believe you walk a religious pathway does not mean there is truth in what you claim or believe.

You see, here we find one the enigmas of true spiritual understanding. You must know yourself to truly understand yourself and to take control over all of the Life Things that you encountered. If you don't truly know yourself, if you are not in control over what you do and what you think and know why you do what you do and think what you think, how can you truly have any control over the deeper reaches of your mind and your true spiritual essence? But, if you focus solely on the external, the outer realms of Inner Mind, you can never find the pathway to letting go of Self. Meaning, you have to know yourself to forget yourself but if all you do is focus on yourself you never let go of the Self.

Ultimately, No Self means No Self. But, how does one get to No Self? As in all things Zen, this is one of the paradoxes of human existence. If you don't know about it, you can't pursue it. If you misunderstand it, you cannot obtain it. But, by wanting it, you have lost the true essence of what it actually is.

So, what are we left with? Desire equals attainment. But, desire is in direct conflict to Śūnyatā. Can you desire Śūnyatā to obtain Śūnyatā? That is the question that you must answer for yourself. But, the one truth of the truth is, as long as you allow yourself to be continually lost in this Life Stuff you will never find a deeper meaning where all of the suffering of life may be overcome, and a true sense of No Self may be experienced.

The simple answer, let go. Can you?

Zen and Enlightenment
09/Jan/2023 02:16 PM

The purpose of Zen is to obtain enlightenment. It is as simple as that. End of story. Yet, throughout the centuries, people have placed all kinds of definitions, schools, practices, and products that are attributed to Zen. Are any of this THINGS a pathway to enlightenment? If they are not, then they are not Zen.

Since the birth of Zen, that evolved from the teachings of Siddhartha Gautama, the Sakyamuni Buddha, enlightenment has been the primary focus of this teaching. Yet, for most, it has become an unachievable goal. Like the pot of gold at the end of the rainbow, it is so close at hand but never obtainable.

The main problem(s) that arises in the pursuit of enlightenment are based in concept. For the few people who actually do choose to devote their life to encountering enlightenment, they each follow a path defined by concept. They are taught the teachings of their teacher and their school. They read the scriptures that have been laid down throughout the centuries. Though all of these things may be understood to be a guide, by their very nature they go against the true understanding of Zen, which is, we all are already enlightened—it is in our ultimate nature. It is only for us to peel back the layers of delusion and illusion for us to perceive this fact. Yet, every word and every teaching, as good intentioned as they may be, do the exact opposite of this. Instead, they add more pieces to the puzzle and make the end goal that much harder to obtain.

There are many facets to Zen that come to the mind of the zealot and the researcher: Zazen or meditation, Dōkyō or reading scriptures, Samu or everyday work done with a spiritual focus, Koan or piecing through the veil and finding the meaning hidden beneath abstract word constructions, and Dentō the passing of enlightenment from teacher to disciple.

These, and many more practices, all define the pathway of Zen. But, they are all just THINGS. And things, by their very nature, keep one from encountering enlightenment. Meaning, hand-in-hand with the essence of Zen, there have intentional roadblocks put up to keep one from obtaining that which is the most easy to obtain if one simply lets go of all of the materializations of the practices.

In Zen, the understanding of, *"Kensho,"* is often explained to be the pathway to nirvana. Kensho means, *"Opening,"* or better explained opening up to the true nature of the Self—that place that is enlightenment. Though some Zen Buddhist sects teach that enlightenment must come via a gradual process following an ever-expanding process of steps and obstacles, this is actually a misunderstanding of the entire truth of Zen. For even if one walks down the road towards finding enlightenment, it is only in that moment when nirvana overcomes the individual where all time and practice is lost to the realms of pure understanding. For once one embraces enlightenment, there is no longer any frame of reference for the pathway that got the individual to that point. All simply is.

For those who walk the pathway of Zen, yes, they are embracing a higher calling. But, just as all inner truths and deep wisdom are hidden behind the veil of illusion, as long as one prefers walking the path to actually obtaining the end goal, there will forever be the need for texts, scriptures, teachers, and schools, that are designed to guide the devotee. But, the truth of the truth of Zen is, that its pinnacle needs no teacher or teaching to obtain. All one has to do is to embrace the pure essence of Zen, located at the root of its teaching and instantly all the schooled stuff become unnecessary. For it is at the point, which by its very definition is the simplest to obtain, enlightenment is known.

If you wish to know about Zen, you can read the books. There are a lot of them out there detailing the understandings of this philosophy. If you want to be called a practitioner of Zen you can go to a temple and be initiated into the sect by a monk. But, if you want to live Zen, then discard all of the physical manifestation and embrace enlightenment, for that is the only true heart of Zen.

Serve Others
08/Jan/2023 02:02 PM

"Every minute you should remember that you are here to serve others. If you are dedicated in life, you have eternal joy and peace," Swami Satchidananda.

I just opened up Facebook to take a quick look at my feed. Like aways, everyone is there posting photos of themselves, advertising this or that, talking about this gig they are going to do, and all that kind of Self-Orientated, Selfish Stuff. Then, I come upon the quote from my teacher, Swami Satchidananda. Don't you think it's kind of a reminder about what we, as human beings, should really be thinking about and actualizing in our life?

Thinking about yourself and doing nothing more than trying to obtain your desires or thinking about helping and serving others, which one do you believe is the better life course?

Making The Roller Blade Seven
06/Jan/2023 03:32 PM

I was recently going through the book I composed about Donald G. Jackson titled: Donald G. Jackson: Soldier of Cinema. As I was perusing the pages and I came upon this chapter, which is actually the first essay I ever wrote about The Roller Blade Seven; composed over twenty years ago. So, for those of you are interested and want to read another take on the creation of the first Zen Film, different from the one that is on this site: The Roller Blade Seven: The Story of the Production, here it is.

Making The Roller Blade Seven
By Scott Shaw

For some reason there has been an ongoing interest in the films *The Roller Blade Seven,* its sequel *Return of the Roller Blade Seven* and the recut, more widely distributed, version of the two films *Legend of the Roller Blade Seven,* sometimes titled *The Legend of the Rollerblade 7,* (which we, the filmmakers, in no way endorse). To this day, almost twenty years since RB7 was released, I still get e-mails and letters from people asking questions about the true meaning of this movie. In other cases, some people have been very critical of this film. But, perhaps that is what is to be expected when you intentionally create a Pure Art Film. Some people just won't get it. In any case, I thought I would write a few words here about the creation of *The Roller Blade* Seven and how it took on a life of its own. To tell the whole story would no doubt fill an entire book. I will try to keep it brief.

First, and perhaps most important, *The Roller Blade Seven* can never be compared to a traditional film. Additionally, it should never be judged by those who wish to compare it to traditional filmmaking, as there was never anything traditional about this movie!

Furthermore, when viewing RB7 and *Return of the Roller Blade Seven* is essential to note that nothing happened randomly—every location, every scene, every segment of dialogue, every visual image, every edit, was a conscious action on the part of Donald G. Jackson and myself.

For those of you who are old enough, or for those of you who have looked back in film history to some of the Avant-garde movies made in the 1960's, *The Roller Blade Seven* is much more on par with those films than the films of today. These films were referred to as, *"Acid Flicks."* This was in reference to the mind-altering drug, LSD. Meaning, they depicted a landscape void of reality. That is perhaps the best way to describe *The Roller Blade Seven*. To bring this comparison up to the modern era, RB7 is much more like an extended Music Video than a film.

As we created RB7, Donald G. Jackson and I very consciously went about making a movie that pushed the envelope of traditional filmmaking. Along the way, several people warned us that we were doing just that and told us that we should stop. Of course, we didn't listen.

Some people have also criticized the acting in *The Roller Blade Seven*. Again, they are really missing the point. Who cares about acting! *The Roller Blade Seven* is about the essence of life—which, in this case, is detailed in the realms of a film. It is not about acting! The only reason any words were spoken at all was to provide some semblance of a story to lure the uninitiated and the unenlightened into the deeper spiritual perspective this film delineates.

Moreover, if anyone looks at the wildness of the characters that make up this film, they will quickly understand that traditional acting has nothing to do with the development and composition of these roles. In fact, it was our intention to push the actors into new areas of expression—the wilder, the more bizarre the acting, the better.

What is a film critic? With very few exceptions, a film critic is someone who wishes they could make a film but does not possess the talent or the dedication to do so.

Pre-Production

Pre-Production for *The Roller Blade* Seven went up in the autumn of 1991. Our offices were located in the Hollywood Center Building on Hollywood Blvd., in Hollywood, California. Quentin Tarantino had just moved out after putting the finishing touches on his directorial debut, *Reservoir Dogs*. Don and I named our Production Company, The Rebel Corp.

Back then, things were very different in Hollywood. If you have seen the film, you will notice that some scenes have upwards of one hundred people on roller blades, sword fighting, etc. All of those people happily worked for free— seeking only a spot in a Hollywood feature film. And, we thank them all.

The First Zen Film

The Roller Blade Seven began shooting on a rainy Saturday morning in November 1991. By the end of the first weekend, Don and I realized that any concept of traditionalism was out the window. We tossed out any predetermined notion we had about the film and simply let spontaneous creativity be our only guide. This was to become the first Zen Film.

For the next several months we shot the film whenever the inspiration struck. We refined the cast as we went along, adding new people as needed.

The story... Don and I didn't care about the story. The stories have all been told!

The Cinematography

For anyone who has the eye to take notice, RB7 possess scope and photographic composition beyond belief. This is in no small part thanks to Don who was a Master Cinematographer.

RB7 was shot on 16mm. The cameras we used were the Aaton S16, the Arri BL, the Bolex Rex 4 with a 24 fps motor, and the 24 fps Canon Scoopic.

The Roller-Cam

While filming RB7 we created a new style of photography. We named it, *"The Roller-Cam."*

We had a masterful skater named Steve Wright who would shoot with Don's Bolex and skate alongside and around the actors. This is what gives many of the scenes in RB7 an ethereal sense of movement. In some scenes, Steve would skate backwards faster than most people can run. The stories I could tell you about some of the amazing things he did while shooting certain segments of RB7...

When people see the footage he shot, they assume we used a camera truck. No, that was just Steve.

For the martial artists who are reading this, there was virtually no choreography. Every fight scene was either completely spontaneous or rehearsed and filmed only once. This occurred due to the fact that 16mm film is not cheap!

The Names

Our Executive Producer had high hopes of making a lot of money on the film. I'm sure she was very disappointed. But, to that end, a few months into production, she had us add several, *"Name,"* players to the film.

Back then, in 1991, if you added known *"Names"* to your film, you could be assured of sales—particularly to foreign markets. Though that is no longer the case, back then, we happily obliged.

Don Stroud

The first inductee was Don Stroud. Don has had an illustrious acting career, including co-starring with Clint Eastwood in *Cogan's Bluff* and *Joe Kidd*. He co-starred in the James Bond film, License to Kill. He also starred in the Motorcycle Cult Classic, Angel Unchained. From my adolescence forward, Don had been one of my favorite actors. So, I was very happy to bring him on board. I had worked with him previously and there is nothing but great things to say about the man. He has remained a close friend.

We drove out to the El Mirage Dry Lake Bed a couple of times with Don and he was nothing but great. You know, he is just one of those masterful actors who UNDERSTANDS. He didn't care that we didn't have a script. He was happy to create his own character.

In fact, in doing so, he became two distinct characters. One was a guardian of The Wheelzone and the second was a conga playing desert dweller. For his second incarnation, we brought along Jill Kelly, (who I will discuss more in a few moments). She and her friend wildly danced around Don as his congas played on.

William Smith

The next inductee was William Smith—also a Clint Eastwood co-star and the ultimate Hollywood Bad Guy.

Another great actor, Bill actually cried when Don and I went to a house in the Hollywood Hills where he was staying to offer him the role.

Back then, Bill liked to drink a lot. He kept his gallon of Vodka close at hand. But, the masterful actor he was, it never slowed him down. His improve was great.

"Can I go home now, Daddy," was his constant mantra.

Karen Black

The next inductee was Golden Globe Winner and Academy Award Nominee, Karen Black. Karen is a sweetheart—a very nice person. Don and I picked her up early one morning at her home in Woodland Hills. She climbed into the back seat of Don's 1962 Plymouth Belvedere and we drove to this Art Farm, which we named, *"The Mushroom Ranch,"* located in the California high-desert. We filmed several scenes with her in a tribute to her Acid Taking Graveyard scene in *Easy Rider*. These scenes became some of the most magical in RB7.

There are no words that could describe the Zen totally of the moments we felt with Karen while we filmed that day.

When I later edited the scenes we shot that day, they came into their own perfection and I truly believe they are visually the high point of the RB7.

Dialogue

Whenever any member of the cast needed words to memorize, we gave them a copy of either *Essence* or *Time*. These are two books that I authored, made up of spiritual aphorisms. The words in these two books make up much of the dialogue of RB7. Karen loved the books and virtually all of her dialogue is based on my writing from those books.

Time was re-worked and re-released in 1999 with the title, *Zen O'clock: Time To Be* and *Essence* was re-released in 2007 with the title, *Essence: The Zen of Everything*.

Don and I bumped into Karen at the twenty-five year reunion screening for the film, *Nashville*. This was held in 2001 at The Academy of Motion Picture Arts and Sciences in Beverly Hills. After the event all of the cast and crew, including: Robert Altman, the director, (who I had worked with on his film, *The Player*), Karen Black, Jeff Goldblum, Keith Carradine, Ronee Blakley, Shelley Duvall, Henry Gibson, Scott Glenn, Lily Tomlin, Cristina Raines, etc., etc.,

etc. went to one of my favorite restaurants, Kate Mantilini's. At the restaurant Karen told us how descendants from the kitten she had brought back from that Art Farm still live with her.

Rhonda Shear

Rhonda Shear was the next *"Name"* cast member to be added to RB7. Rhonda is a very sweet, flirtatious lady. At the time she was in RB7 she was hosting a late-night T.V. show called *Up All Night.* This show broadcast weird art-house moves on the USA Network. A couple of Don's films regularly showed on the program and I am sure the reason the Executive Producer wanted her in the film was so RB7 would also appear on the USA Network. Though the original *Roller Blade Seven* was never shown on *Up All Night*, *Legend of the Roller Blade Seven* was broadcast several times.

Frank Stallone

The next cast member added was Frank Stallone. The previous *"Name"* talents were all cool beyond belief. Frank, well that was a bit different story…

We had Frank meet us at the Granada Hills home of one of the film's A.C.'s (Camera Assistants). We then loaded him into Don's car and headed for the location.

"Are the crew waiting for us at the location," Frank asked. Don and I laughed because he and I were the crew.

The Crew

During the filming of RB7 Don operated the camera; I did the sound. So, the process was, I would get the DAT up and running, Don would roll the camera, then I would go into frame with the slate, call the scene, slap the slate, walk out, then walk back in and act.

Needless to say, through Frank acted out his part and behaved like a true professional, he did not see the ART in that process.

De Soto Jungle

We took Frank to this location we had dubbed, *"De Soto Jungle."* There we shot the encounter between his character and mine where we battle with Samurai Swords.

It is hard to forget the look on Frank's face when Don handed him the rubber Black Knight suite we had picked up for him. His embarrassment radiated and I am sure he was wondering was the $6,000.00 we were paying him for one day of work worth it. None-the-less, he put on the suit and we shot the scenes.

It is important to note that on film we knew the suit would look fine. In the up-close-and-personal, however, it did look kind of fake.

A funny story involving Frank occurred after we filmed our first scenes with him and had returned to our AC's house. Don looked at me with fear in his eyes and said, *"What are we going to have Frank say?"* I suggested we go for a ride, which we did. We ended up at Tommy Burgers in the North Valley. We had a couple of burgers and etched out the basis of what Frank would say.

We returned to the garage of our AC, where Mark Richardson had constructed our sets. Filming continued…

Joe Estevez

The final *"Name"* talent to be added was Joe Estevez. Joe, perhaps best known for being the brother of Martin Sheen, is a great guy and has remained a close friend—who I have worked with several times.

Don and I had not met Joe prior to shooting with him that first night. But, we had seen him in the film *Soultaker*. This is the film that led Joe to indie film stardom.

The shoot was planned for stages had set up at our Hollywood office building. We also had a dressing room set aside for Joe. When he arrived, we lead him to it. But, Joe being Joe would have nothing to do with it. He just wanted to hang out.

Joe's a great actor. Like Karen Black, much of his dialogue in RB7 came from my two books, *Essence* and *Time*.

David Carradine and Erik Estrada

Don and I courted both David Carradine and Erik Estrada to be in RB7. I had worked with David in another film and, if nothing else, he is an interesting guy. To this day, his original *Kung Fu* T.V. Series remains one of the most important events in television history.

Don and I had both previously worked with Eric. So, we went to his house and discussed the role he would play. We had a pink Harley Davidson lined up for his character—playing off of his role on television series *CHIP's*.

Both David and Eric were up for doing the movie. But, due to contractual difficulties, brought about by the Executive Producer, neither of them appeared in the film.

Jill Kelly

Some people have noticed that we used a few Adult Film Stars in RB7. This is true. Jade East was in the film and Jill Kelly's first role on film was in this movie. To name just a few...

We had meet Jill, then known by her given name Adrianne Moore, through a friend of Don's who was a dancer in a strip club in Bakersfield, California—where Adrianne also worked. The four of us went out and had a great time getting drunk on margaritas in a Burbank, California hot spot.

For those of you in other parts of the country and the world, Burbank is the home of many of the major film and

T.V. studios. So, a lot of industry people hang out around the city.

We hit it off right away and we asked Jill to be in the film. From the time we first meet her forward, I have nothing but nice things to say about Jill. She is super-professional and a very nice person.

After her appearance in RB7 she went on to become one of the top players in the Adult Film Industry. Don and I have worked with her a few times since RB7. And, she has remained a very nice person.

Traci Lords

Perhaps the saddest thing about the *"Name"* talent that was to be associated with RB7 was the loss of Traci Lords.

We heard Traci was looking for a new project. I had not worked with Traci before but Don had worked with her on the film *Shock 'em Dead*. So, she was offered the role of the female lead.

Traci, particular about the films she worked on, came by to look at some footage from RB7 with her agent. We met at EZTV, when it was located on Santa Monica Blvd. in West Hollywood. She liked what she saw—all the flamboyance and radical cinematography. She *"Got on the Bus,"* as we used to say.

Traci came by our offices the next day and wanted to know about her character. I silently laughed as Don attempted to explain that this was *Zen Filmmaking* and we simply allowed spontaneous creation to be our only guide. *"What, no script!"* Don handed her copies of my two aforementioned books and told her she could use any passage she wanted from them. Though not completely satisfied, she agreed.

One of the things that really impressed me about Traci was the fact that she understood her character was going to wield a Samurai Sword in the film. She wanted to look professional. So, each afternoon she would come by, we would go onto our back stages, and I would teacher her proper Samurai techniques. We gave her a Samurai Sword to practice with at home and each day she would come back having mastered the previous day's techniques. Few actors or actresses, take their roles this seriously—especially for an independent production.

Traci even re-dyed her hair blonde for the film—as per Don's request. This, just after she had taken it to a strawberry blonde. So, she was really up for the project.

The day came to sign the contract. Our Executive Producer, looking to her own future, had devised a contract that stated she could use any footage filmed for RB7 in any additional movie she desired—from here to eternity... Traci, obviously a savvy businesswoman, was not going to become Stock Footage and would not sign the contract. All she wanted was that wording be taken out. The Executive Producer would not budge.

Perhaps the most unfortunate thing about this situation was that I was the one elected to give Traci her contract. So, she blamed me. I received an understandably very angry phone call from her the night all this took place, stating, *"You're the Producer of this project—do something!"* But, I was not the one providing the financing. So, there was nothing I could do. Sadly, we lost Traci Lords.

But, back to the story line...

Return Of the Roller Blade Seven

During the filming of *The Roller Blade Seven* we realized that one film was just not enough to cover the entire subject matter of Artistic Filmmaking and Cinematic Enlightenment that we wanted to present. Don and I were sitting down, having a burger, at Jay Burgers over on Virgil and Santa Monica in East Hollywood and we had a revelation—we needed to make two films. As Don had a contract for two films with our Executive Producer, we decided that the best thing to do was to create a second feature in association with RB7. Thus, was born *Return of the Roller Blade Seven.* With this film we decided to present an even more artistic landscape and provide clues and answers to some of the Cinematic Zen Koans presented in the first film. For this reason, if anyone wishes to truly understand what we were trying to do with RB7, the second film must also be studied.

More Gold

Upon the completion of filming each day we took our film to the lab to be developed. After we picked it up, we would head over to a Telecine house in Burbank, where a great Colorist named, Wilks Butler, did our color correction for us.

"MG," was the word, *"More Gold."* Don and I were both in love with the look of The Golden Hour, (the hour just before sunrise and just after sunset), and we attempted to make RB7 look as gold as possible.

Some of my fondest memories of RB7 are the hours, leading to days; we spent in Telecine on RB7. Wilks would have his runner Alex go and get us Chili from *Chili John's* in Burbank and we would eat while we watched RB7.

Magical Things

Many magical events occurred during the creation of RB7. One of the most striking was the fact that Don and I decided to go and have some Production Stills developed at this shop in Burbank. Inside, the walls were lined with photos of this one very beautiful girl. We asked about her. The story was, the shop had a photo day and she was the model. Looking at this girl's photos, I could not help but think, *"I would really like to meet her."* About an hour later, Don and I stopped at a 711. Inside, a girl walked up to me and said, *"You look like a rock star."* Low-and-behold, it was the same girl.

Hard to believe, but very true. We gave her the role of Sister Sparrow in the film and she became one of the female leads.

Editing

Editing is where RB7 took shape. We began in a traditional manner—hiring the editor who had edited Don's film, Roller Blade to work while Don and I supervised. The editor made two big mistakes:

1. He just did not understand Art.
2. He taught me how to use the equipment.

I edited, while he would sit there and try to make sense out of the movie.

A Funny Story

One of the interesting things that occurred, that perhaps heralded our leaving the realms of traditional editing, was that while we were attempting to get the original editor to understand our style of *Zen Filmmaking*—one morning, upon arriving at the Sunset Boulevard building where the editing studio was located, Don went to the bathroom. With him he carried all of our DAT tapes.

We had recorded the sound for RB7 on the, (then), newly developed DAT (Digital Audio Technology) format.

Don left the bathroom with the tapes sitting on the sink. Once in the editing studio he soon realized what he had done and we quickly returned to get them. But, they were gone. We had hoped someone had just picked them up for safekeeping. So, we went and asked, suite-to-suite. But, to no avail. We put up a notice in the bathroom, but no one ever responded.

That's Hollywood for you. Had it not been for the fact that we had transferred all of our Beta Master Sources Tapes to 3/4 inch for editing, during Telecine, we would have had no audio for the films. It was as if some guardian angel was looking out for us…

The Editing Moves

Don and I quickly realized that the original editor was not the man for the job. We rented an editing suite at Midtown Video, across the street for the Beverly Center, and I went to work.

Never to live the life of traditionalism—while I edited RB7, we also cast upcoming features. There were times in that editing suite when we had upwards of twenty beautiful would-be Hollywood starlets hanging out and hanging on; willing to do whatever it takes to get a role in a film.

A friend of Don's came by one particular evening. In disbelief, he asked, *"Does stuff like this really happen?"* Yes, it does.

One More Time

People often comment about the multiple takes we repeatedly show in RB7. The reason for this is based in two unique perspectives. The first is, I decided to take the multiple angle cuts, which were being used in the martial art films of the late 1980's and early 1990's, to the next level. Let's give the audience, *"In Your Face ART."* I could go on and on about why. But, it is as simple as that... Art for art sake.

The second, more metaphysical, reasoning is that I was referencing that altered state of reality which occurs when you take hallucinogenic drugs—sometimes your mind flashes back over the same image several times. Though, in reality, it is the same. It, none-the-less, appears to be quite different and quite unique each time it is studied.

During the editing I would often look over at Don while I edited and ask, *"What do you think?"* after having laid in one, two, or three flash cuts. He would smirk, shake his head, *"Yes,"* and say, *"One, two, maybe three more."*

Though *The Roller Blade Seven* was the first film I ever edited, when I look at it today, I believe it is some of my best work. Don Jackson never stopped talking about how much he loved the edit on RB7.

There was no precise technique that I used while editing the film. As is always the case with *Zen Filmmaking*, I simply allowed the moment to guide me and what came out was Art.

People often ask me why I have never edited another film in the style of RB7. You have to understand, when I edited RB7, this was before all of the effects, multiple screens, and color variations that came hand-in-hand with the digital revolution. All I had to work with was the film. I feel what I did with RB7 made the statement I wanted to make at that point in history. With all of the technology that has occurred since that point in time, what I did back then has since become very easy—it has become commonplace. You can see it on all the trendy T.V. shows.

Me, I have moved on. Though I will occasionally reference a moment of RB7 editing in my later films, all the flash cuts, and mismatched frame edits of RB7 have become so common, so expected that now I am working from a different space of consciousness.

All the Rage

Don, who possessed a volatile temper, occasionally would go into a rage about various things while we edited. At one point, he got so mad he smashed his fist into the wall of our editing suite, breaking his hand. He went to the doctor. I continued to edit.

Dark Days

By the time Don and I took RB7 and *Return of the Roller Blade Seven* to Rick Spalla Productions in Hollywood to create the final master copies of the films, we had hit dark days. Don, being one of the greatest squanders of money I have ever known, (and I say that as a compliment), had spent our Production Budget and our Executive Producer had cut off any further funding. So, we were flat broke. This situation was amplified by the fact that my 1964 Porsche 356 SC had blown its transmission and fixing it was not going to be cheap. So, I was delegated to riding my Harley Davidson to the Post-Production sessions—many times in the pouring rain. Finances got so bad I had to sell my 1930's D'Angelico New Yorker guitar, simply to survive. For any of you who understand the value and rarity of these instruments, (basically, they are the Stradivarius of guitars), you can understand our plight. But, like the spiritual transformation presented in RB7—good overpowering evil, we continued to fight the good fight.

Though it was unplanned, I ended up doing the soundtrack for the two films, as well. This was mostly motivated by budgetary considerations.

I had spent my entire life as a musician. So, this was really no problem. The only downside, I only had one weekend, (two days), to compose and perform it all. And, this was prior to computer integration into music.

Plus, we planned to have music in every-single scene. So, it was not going to be easy...

I wanted the soundtrack for the two films to possess a very rhythmic-tribal vibe. The only problem was, my drum machine died just prior to my beginning the soundtracks. The situation was saved by a sweet, beautiful Chinese girl, via Hawaii, who had befriended me just prior to the beginning of RB7's production. She went to Guitar Center in Hollywood and bought me a new drum machine—which saved the soundtrack. I think I still owe her the money for it. *"Thank you Laurie!"*

Though it was not an easy accomplishment, with a little help from Mike Spalla, our On-Line Engineer, we finished the soundtracks and the films. When the two films were completed, we knew we had created works of Pure Art. Not commercial filmmaking. But, ART!

The Release of Roller Blade Seven

RB7 and *Return of the Roller Blade Seven* were released at the 1992 American Film Market (AFM). European countries were the first to purchase the rights. Don and I never saw a dime.

Little fanfare occurred upon the release of these films. This was in no small part due to marketing decisions made by the Executive Producer—which Don and I had nothing to do with. So, I began to send copies of RB7 out to the various industry magazines and to some industry professionals. If nothing else, it did get noticed.

If I may reiterate, it is important to note that to truly understand the message of spiritual evolution presented in *The Roller Blade Seven,* one must also view *Return of the Roller Blade Seven.* We made these movies hand-in-hand. And, though they each possess a unique and specific spiritual message, to understand the complete process of Zen Cinematic Enlightenment, one must view them both. This, however, immediately became nearly impossible once the Executive Producer took possession of them.

Stabbed in the Back

Soon after the 1992 AFM, as is so often the case in Hollywood, we the filmmakers: Donald G. Jackson and I got backstabbed. The Executive Producer decided the two features would market better as a single film. So, without telling us, she broke all our contracts and had the films reedited, titling it *Legend of the Roller Blade Seven.*

When one views *Legend of the Roller Blade Seven,* in comparison to *The Roller Blade Seven* and *Return of the Roller Blade Seven,* one can truly see the ineptitude of the Re-Editors. They simply took scenes I had edited from the original features and combined them into one film. Oftentimes, they misaligned the music hits which we had added to the original films. So, several visual situations occur and the hit goes off either too soon or too late. They also added some bad narration. The Executive Producer also deleted many of our cast and crew credits—most notably my Producer credit. Basically, our vision was destroyed. As such, in no way do we endorse the version of the film *Legend of the Roller Blade Seven,* sometimes titled *Legend of the Rollerblade 7*—though this is the version which was released in the U.S. and is much easier to find.

But, it wasn't just Don and myself. While we were still casting the film, prior to shooting, a very nice girl came in, Allison Chase. She became, Stella Speed, the female lead of the two films. And, she can be seen featured in many of the film's photos. She was a real trooper, hanging out throughout the long production. Don and I gave her the *"Introducing"* credit in RB7, as this was her first film role, and second billing in *Return of the Roller Blade Seven.* But, her name was virtually wiped from the history of *Roller Blade* by the Executive Producer. It was very sad to see Allison's reaction to being excommunicated from RB7. But, there was nothing Don or I could do about it. The good news is Allison has gone on to win a Grammy Award for her work as a producer on a reality based T.V. show.

This is an important lesson to all actors, actresses, and filmmakers—be careful whom you work with in Hollywood, because the money has the power, and the power can do anything that it wants.

The Roller Blade Seven Trilogy

Initially, Don Jackson and I planned to make a series of three feature films in association with *The Roller Blade Seven.* This was to be known as *The Roller Blade Seven Trilogy.* This intended trilogy was in direct reference to the holy trinity of the Christian and Hindu religions.

We completed the first two of the trilogy…

Some people have mistakenly assumed that *Legend of the Roller Blade Seven* was the third installment of *The Roller Blade Seven Trilogy*. This is incorrect. The third film was to be titled *Wheelzone Rangers*. Though we intended to make this film, and a few times actually attempted to bring it up. But, this never came to be, prior to the passing of Don Jackson (RIP).

This is a film I still plan to make, however. At the appropriate time, when the necessary inspiration, financing, and cast are in place, Hawk Goodman, (my character), will reappear in The Wheelzone.

Moving On

Virtually immediately after the 1992 AFM, I began filming *Samurai Vampire Bikers from Hell*. The Executive Producer of RB7, true to her nature, had my cast and crew thrown out of our Hollywood office building and stages on the first day of shooting. This was obviously very uncool, especially after the months of undaunted effort I had put into RB7. Her actions were amplified by the fact that a large part of the time I worked on RB7, I did so without pay. But, in the long run, it was the best thing that could have happened to my production and to me.

My friends Ken Kim, Vince Spezze and I packed up the equipment. Vince and I then went to a strip club and got drunk. As if a veil of negativity had been lifted, I was free from all of the darkness that had haunted the production of RB7. I never returned to the Hollywood Center Building. I brought *Samurai Vampire Bikers from Hell* back up and finished it a short time later.

Don and I had begun playing around with the newly released Hi-8 format near the end of RB7's production. I loved the ease of the format. An actress, Susan Jay, who I had meet while we were doing some final casting for RB7, purchased a Sony CCD V5000 camera for me—which became my main production tool for my next two films.

Don, inspired by my immersion into the Hi-8 format, went on to do his own video features. We did not work together again until 1995.

To some people, RB7 and *Return of the Roller Blade Seven* are weird or strange. To us, that is good. These films were created with Spirituality and Art as their central focus. And, true Spirituality and Art are never normal, known, or truly understood.

Like I always say, *"You may not like the ART of Picasso but you cannot say it is not ART!"* This is how I feel about RB7.

For myself, even to this day, I laugh whenever I watch these two films. The same was true of Don before his passing.

Sure, there is a lot of inside humor in *The Roller Blade Seven* and *Return of the Roller Blade Seven*. Sure, they are cinematically self-indulgent. Sure, they project an artistic landscape only truly understood by we, the filmmakers. But, it is essential to understand; *"Fun is what they are both all about."*

As it is taught in Zen, if you can remove yourself from the constrains of reality, enlightenment is found. These two films are designed to be like the Zen Koan, a subtle way to step beyond the realms of reality and embrace Nirvana.

The Zen

Mṛtyu and Forty-Nine Days to Nirvana
05/Jan/2023 10:11 AM

I was driving to have breakfast with my lady this morning. Where I live, sometimes the clouds can get very-very thick. So much so that there have been times when I could barely see the front of my car. Due to the atmospheric river rainstorm we are currently undergoing, the visibility was just a little bit better than that this AM.

As we drove, we were discussing the various situations we have encountered during these types of conditions. Just then, I see a minivan, in the slow lane, literally stopped. I have no idea what, when, or why they were doing that but I did understand that if they do not move someone is going to run into them fairly soon. I don't know, maybe that's what they want???

As we drove on, I told the story of the first time I had ever encountered driving conditions like this. It was in the Hollywood Hills near Laurel Canyon and my friend and I were doing what sixteen year old teenagers do, driving around in their car. Many of the streets in the Hollywood Hills are very-very small. Even when it is clear, you have to drive very carefully. But, there, then, I could barely see to the front of my hood. My friend was hanging out of the passenger window, just to help me navigate.

Then I said, *"You know, he doesn't even remember that?"* My lady immediately climes in, *"Because he's dead!"* She's always been kind of harsh like that. Yes, that was my friend who, as I've discussed in this blog, passed-away a couple of months ago.

It's kind of weird the memories that come to mind of a friend or family member who recently passed-away. Memories that you may not have even thought about had they not been churned up in your mind because of their passing.

In Sanskrit, the word, *"Mṛtyu,"* is used to describe death. In Hinduism, the deity Māra is the goddess of death. In Buddhism this same name is assigned to a god who symbolizes death leading to rebirth. In other sects, this personage is viewed as a demon of death.

All this being stated, the fact of the fact is, people pass on from their physical existence. Sad but true. We are all going to die. But, then what? Some religions are really great, they promise if you are good then you will go to heaven. Isn't being good always a good thing? But, how many people would truly pass the muster of being deemed as having been wholly good in their life? None, I believe, if all were judged honestly. So, who's in heaven?

In Buddhism, it is believed that it takes forty-nine days from the time a person dies for their essence, spirit, and being to be released into the cosmos where they may then either reenter the cycle of reincarnation or, if they were spiritually pure, find nirvana. I don't know if that timeframe is truly exact, but from my experience, when someone I know has died, I have encountered their energy, blessings, and gifts from the great beyond for a least a short amount of time. So, them being somewhere between the here and the there, for a time, seems probable. But, how can we truly know? How can anyone truly know?

In Buddhism, it is understood that it is the clinging and the desire that holds one bound to this physical plane. Perhaps those that have loved life the most are those who hold most fervently to this place we know as life. Perhaps it is those who have loved the most, loved someone the most, they are the ones who do not want to let go. I know I had this one cat that passed away, many years ago now, and for a long time after she moved on I would feel her energy in our apartment every now and then. She was the only furry friend I ever felt that energy from after they had moved on. So???

But then, knowing this and believing that, there have been those I have known who have passed away and I have felt nothing. They were just gone. So, who's to say?

Ideas about what happens after death have been spoken about since the dawning of life. But, life is life and that is all we know. So, all we can define anything by is our own understanding of life. ...Knowing what we know based upon what we have lived.

People and all other living entities move on and away from that which we experience as life. We will too. It is only then that will be able to put a clear and precise definition onto what actually happens after our physical being is no more. The only problem being, then it will be too late. We will be dead. Thus, all that will be left of the life that we lived is the memories that others hold of us. What memories will other people hold of you?

* * *
04/Jan/2023 03:31 PM

Did you do the right thing?

All Things Are a Manifestations of Your Mind
04/Jan/2023 08:12 AM

What are you thinking about right now? What brought you to this page to read this writing? What were you doing before you came here? What will you do after? After reading these questions, will you simply change the page and go somewhere else so you can think about something else?

It is understood in both Hindu and Buddhist philosophy that all things you encounter in your life are nothing more than a manifestation of your mind. From a Hindu perspective, this understanding goes deeper in stating that the world is actually a projection of your mind. Your essence, that soul within you, (by whatever name you want to label it), is projecting all things outwards. Thus, you are creating your reality.

The Buddhist perspective is not so self-defining as that. But, it does state that you, and your thoughts, are what creates your reality.

All you have to do is to look at the encounters of your life and you can quickly see this to be true. What did you do yesterday that brought you to this moment right here, right now?

Certain things you do in your life have vast consequences. Look to something large, grand, or catastrophic that occurred to you. How did you get to that point in your life? Was it not you having a desire that caused you to do one thing that led to another? The answer is obvious.

Other events seem more forced upon you. …Someone did something to you that was against what you ever hoped or wished for. But, if you look deeper into those occurrences, was it not you who made a choice that placed yourself in that environment where that doing could be done to you?

Most people never consider any of this. They just do. If what they do makes them happy, all is well with their world. If what they do makes them unhappy, how many look to their own fault in the situation? Instead, most simply look for someone else to blame. But, it is your fault!

In Sanskrit, the word, *"Prakṛti,"* describes the physical and emotional realms of reality. This is the Mind-Place where human nature, intellect, ego, morality, and human desire dwells. This is where we, as human beings, exist. This is where all action leads to reaction. This is also the realm where one may take control over their mind and their mind-based desires and focus on living a pure and conscious existence. But, who does this? How few are the people who live in a space of refined consciousness? At best, some claim to try to exist on this plane. Others may even claim they possess the ability to do so. But, do they? Is claiming anything ever based in truth? Or, is that just Mind Junk? Truth is only prevalent in the individual who claims nothing.

In some schools of thought, they teach that Prakṛti is the place that keeps the individual from encountering liberation. But again, isn't that a choice?

The Sanskrit term, *"Purusha,"* advanced during the early evolution of Hinduism. This word describes Self in association with the Cosmic Inner Being. It is believed that this is the place where one must embrace if they hope to rise above the limitations of thoughtless choice.

So, back to the point of this piece. Where do you exist? How did you get to this place in your life? What level of Mind are you allowing to control your actions defining where you find yourself in your life? How will the actions you choose to undertake today affect your tomorrow and perhaps more importantly, how will the actions you choose to take today affect the life of someone else's tomorrow?

All life is your choice. What do you choose to do with that choice? What will you manifest?

You can walk through your life in the most meaningless, unrefined manner possible, if that is what you choose to do. But remember, that is a choice. If that is your choice, what you do equals what you experience. So, don't blame anyone else for what your karma makes you encounter.

What do you hope to experience in your life? Chaos and karma or enlightenment?

Wake Up!
03/Jan/2023 08:13 AM

It was a cold, rainy day. The rain had stopped for a while, and I was walking along the sidewalk in this SoCal beach community. Up ahead I could see there was this young-ish homeless guy. He was obviously suffering from some sort of mental illness. As I walked closer, he saw me coming and kind of got out of the way. Just as I passed him, he smashed the shrubbery that lined the sidewalk with a small branch he had in his hand and yelled, *"Wake up!"* I looked, thinking that maybe he was trying to wake up his pet or something, but there was nothing there. Just some image locked only in his own mind.

The thing is, his yelling, *"Wake up,"* really woke me up. I mean, it was not so loud or intense to make me think I needed to go into fight mode or anything like that. It was just loud enough to cause me to Wake Up.

This is one of those Life Things. We all just kind of pass through it. Sure, like in a situation like I was in: at a very scenic location, hearing the waves, the temperature was cool and invigorating, and the air was very clean and clear as it had just rained. But, though we may like or even love what we are feeling, how present are we? For most, myself included, yeah I was liking what I was experiencing, but was I really there? Was I one hundred percent in my moment? No. But, by that guy exclaiming, *"Wake up,"* it really brought me into my moment. It made me one hundred precent present. It is in those moment of Full Presence that life is truly experienced.

The thing is, the abstract life events that bring you fully into your moment cannot be charted. You don't know when they are going to happen. And, telling yourself, I really need to stay present is a great thing. But, just telling yourself that does not make it happen. At least not for more than a few moments. So, what can you do to become fully present?

First of all, you have to want it. You have to understand the benefit and the reason why. To truly understand that, you must have experienced it. Have you? Have you experienced being fully present? If you have then you know exactly what I'm speaking about. If you have not, you should try it.

You probably can't get the full impact of it if you are reading this at your computer or something. If this is the case, just hold the thought until you are maybe outside, maybe in a quiet space, or something like that. Then, let go. Totally, let go. STOP. Allow all things to be as all things are. Don't run from anything—any thought, feeling, or experience. Just allow it and the everything to be.

The feeling of being Totally Present is different for everyone. So, I'm not going to try to describe it to you here. It is your feeling, you feel it. But, once you have experienced it, you will know why it is an enhanced state of consciousness.

You can do the exercise of choosing to be Totally Present whenever you want. The more you do it, the more you will choose to do it. The thing is, life takes hold of us all. We forget that we should be present. So, maybe you can do something like set the alarm on your watch or your phone for whatever random time(s) you feel will be ideal. Then, forget about it until that chime chimes. Immediately, when it does, let go. Let that be your, *"Wake up,"* moment.

Being Totally Present really allows you to experience life on a whole new level in a whole new way.

Try it. Wake Up!

Kittens, Rainbows, and Śuddha
31/Dec/2022 08:36 AM

Pretty much every religion and Self-Help Guru will tell you that you must have pure thoughts if you hope to live a good, karma-free, enlightened life, and rise your mind to higher levels of consciousness. Let's face facts, most couldn't care less about this ideology. How many people do you know that actually try to practice Good Thought? Do you?

For those who do walk the spiritual path, however, they may try to shove negative thoughts, sexual fantasies, and anything else that they believe to be wrong or of lower consciousness from their brain. But, push as they may, thoughts will come back. Why? Because we are all schooled to think in a certain manner. We do not live in a truly spiritual society where all aspire to the most high. Thus, all around us we are consciously bombarded with less than pure thoughts and trained to walk down a road of impurity. For those who do choose the path of Right Thought, they must constantly fight not only the negative thoughts which emulate from their own mind but all of the taunting of those who believe they are foolish in attempting to follow a higher calling.

Think about your life and your life experiences for a moment. When are you the happiest? My guess would be, you are the happiest when you are quietly doing something simple that makes you feel good. Maybe it is meditating, maybe it's gardening, maybe it is painting or drawing, maybe it's cooking, maybe it's surfing a wave, maybe it's doing Hatha Yoga or Tai Chi, maybe it is petting your furry friend. There/then you can happy, calm, and of a pure mind with the most simple of accessories.

It is important to understand there is a big difference between a peaceful happiness and adrenalized agitation. The ladder may well make you feel more alive, more empowered, more invigorated—which leads some to believe this is happiness. But, in that moment of excitement, where are your thoughts? Are they in and of the Higher Self? Or, are they lost to the agitation that is brought about by whatever it is that is causing you to feel that way? Moreover, once that feeling has left you, what are you left with? A Higher Mind? No. Just an absence of excitement. Thus, re-seeking whatever it is that caused you to feel that emotion become a desired drug and this, by its very nature, is not a definition of Higher Mind.

So, where does leave us? It tells us that it must be you, the individual, who chooses to focus your mind on obtaining a spiritual sense of purity if you wish to truly become part of higher consciousness. How do you do that? The easiest way is to not make it complicated. Don't beat yourself if you think a negative thought. Just don't let yourself act on it. Catch yourself, refocus your mind on something positive. And mostly, find and develop things and activities in your life that keep you mentally in a spiritual place. Whatever that spiritual place may be, it will be discovered in the simple: in the garden, walking in the mountains or along the shore, embracing the easy, the natural, and the pure.

You don't have to fight yourself to be mentally pure, you simply must choose a positive focus.

Remember, you do not have to live the life that most people embrace, being dominated by all that stuff that causes them/you to develop negative karma. You can be more, you can be more pure. Just find that place within yourself where negative thoughts and desires don't direct you down an undesirable road and haunt your consciousness. In that place of simple simplicity, Pure Mind can be experienced. Once it has been known, you will know why it has been detailed throughout time as the best pace to exist.

Free your mind of hurtful thoughts and you will be free.

* * *
30/Dec/2022 02:08 PM

As long as you believe someone has something they can give to you, you will always be disappointed with them when you don't receive it.

Direct Cinema and The Perfect Sound
30/Dec/2022 08:05 AM

  In some case, the most simply things can create great art. Yes, there is the long and elaborate creations that take forever to actualize. And, some of them are very good. The one thing that art created by that method has, however, is the obviousness of its actualization. Other times, it is the most simple and natural method that creates art that holds its own perfection without attempting to follow a path that takes way too much time, effort, money, and does not promise to end in anything more perfect. Think about it…

  I was flipping channels last night, as I tend to do, as my night was winding down. …I know I've been saying that a lot lately here in this blog. But, that's how life is, isn't it? There are times in your life when certain things and/or certain life activities repeat themselves.

  Anyway, I flipped on the great movie, *The Doors,* (really sad what happened to Val Kilmer in his life, but I think it was great that they gave him a role in *Top Gun Maverick*). I turned it on just at the point when his character, Jim Morrison, was saying, *"No one does Direct Cinema anymore."* It really got me to thinking how essential that style of cinema is to the overall development of the craft. I know it is one of my primary practices. But, how many people even understand what *Direct Cinema* is? Think of all the critics and reviewers out there who throw shade on all the indie filmmakers, yet they do not even understand the basis of their art—the pure simplicity of their art.

  If you don't know the origin of the art, how can you understand the art? If you don't know the foundation of the art form, how can you critique the art form?

  After that I popped over to the CW network. The song from Lady Antebellum, who became Lady A to stay politically correct, *"What If I Never Get Over You,"* came on. That's one of those songs that just knocks me for a loop every time I hear it. I mean, the sound production on that song is just exquisite. It's like when you go back to *The Wall of Sound* developed by Phil Spector, which I was never a particular fan of, and take it to a whole new level of audio excellence. Just perfect.

Whether you like that style of music or not I suggest you check that song out and simply listen to audio its excellence.

With that, I then had to switch over to YouTube and listen to and watch some of my favorites. You know, just to get a dose of what I consider that audio rightness.

For the Record: In my music, mostly I hear the What-is-Not, but in a few cases, in a few songs, I feel like I achieved this satori of audio okay-ness.

So, here's the thing… You can make everything complicated, critiquing all that you don't understand or haven't taken the time to learn the foundations and the origin of. As Dylan said, all those years ago, *"…Don't criticize what you can't understand."* Or, you can be Mind Free enough to let the perfection fall where it falls—live where it lives. Life/Art does not need to be something based in complicated expansion; it can be allowed to be free—to be simple. In fact, isn't that the best art; the most pure? The free and the simple? Think about that the next time you experience one of those moment of sound or cinematic satori. Those points when you just allow life and the art to be as it is as you are overcome with that perfect feeling of rightness.

Direct Cinema!

The Headshot Paradox
AKA Appearances Are Deceiving
28/Dec/2022 02:20 PM

For anyone who has ever entered the acting game you know that your headshot is your ticket to getting a role in a film or on TV. Without a headshot you cannot do anything.

From this and because of this, the headshot is the first thing that an actor is expected to get when they come to Hollywood. After that, they send out those headshots to production companies who have issued casting notices and to agent in hopes of getting representation.

Of course, the moment you go to see an agent and they agree to represent you, they will give you all of the reasons that they do not like your current headshot and they will send you out to get new headshots done by a photographer they recommend. I won't go into the whole why and wherefore of that, just know that is part of the game.

As a producer, the positive element of dealing with an agent is, you at least kind of know what you are going to get with an actor. I mean, they oversee the headshot situation, and they only send out a headshot that actually represents their client.

I have told this story in a lot of places before, both as a warning to filmmakers and a thing to keep in mind for the actor, a lot of people look nothing like their headshot. I cannot tell you how many times someone has showed up at my production office with a headshot they either had taken twenty years ago or one that was so altered it looked nothing like them. I always exclaim, *"I want to meet the person in this picture."*

Back in the day, headshots were all sent out via snail mail. Even me, I used to spend a lot of money on stamps in order to get an audition. The agents they had their runners, but they also did snail mail, as well. Now, it's all electronic, which makes the whole process not only cheaper but a whole lot easier. This being stated, you are still not sure what you may possibly get in-person based on a headshot.

I know I've told you this story at least once, but a few years back I was contacted by an agent who wanted to discuss representing me. Okay, sure, let's see what we see. I showed up at their office and they asked for my headshot. What? *"I have tons but they're all online." "We like to see real headshots,"* said the lady sub-agent. I smiled, said, *"Thanks,"* turned and walked out the door. Way too Old School for me. Of course, as a means of some sort of retribution, (I guess), the agent called up my manager and talked all kinds of shit about me on her voicemail. She may have called my current agent, as well, but I never heard anything about that. Awh, Hollywood...

But, before I get too far off target here... I was at AFM a number of years ago. I was just taking a moment, standing on the mezzanine balcony, looking out over all the goings-on. This was back when AFM was still a thing, before the internet robbed the world of all of its personal contact. Anyway, I notice this woman going up to people and passing out her headshot. She walked up to me, handed me her headshot, and started to give me her spiel. Immediately, I saw that she looked nothing like her headshot. The one she handed me made her like someone somewhere in her twenties when she obviously, at that point, well in her early forties. She looked down at the badge I was wearing and she saw it was Press Badge. I had a couple different badges at that AFM. I was wearing my Press Badge, at the moment, because it allowed to get into a few things that a Seller's Badge did not. Anyway, seeing that, she took her headshot out of my hand and gave me some snide comment like unless I wanted to write an article about her, I could do nothing for her career. Inside, all this made me laugh. It also made me want to say, *"Fuck off."* Here she was, someone with no credits, a headshot that didn't even look like her, playing the Hollywood game, and expecting all the doors to be opened for her for no reason. How typical, I thought.

She walked away, her headshot in hand. I stood there shaking my head.

The funny thing about all this is, about a week or so after the market, I was casting a new film. Who's headshot did I get? Yes, you guessed it. The aforementioned woman.

My first thought was to call her in. You know, just to let her know how she should not have been so judgmental. But, I knew with an attitude like hers, I would never want to work with her so why waste my time. I just smilingly tossed her headshot into the No-Go pile.

But, this is an essential thing that you should think about as you pass through life. One: Are you presenting you with an honest portrayal of who and what you truly are? Two: Are you letting people into your life who are not what they portray themselves to be? In this world of the internet, where in many cases you never interact with someone face-to-face, who are you really dealing with and how are you being deceived? You really need to think about this stuff. You really need to be honest about yourself. You really need to be prepared for a person not being what they claim to be.

Reality is only as true as who you are living your reality with.

The Art and the Craft of Filmmaking
28/Dec/2022 09:21 AM

I was kicking back last night, with a nice bottle of Sangiovese, watching the movie *Super Fly* on TCM. The original 1972 release of this film.

Of course, I have seen this film so many times. I remember the first time I saw at the Wiltern Theater, here in Los Angeles, when it was first released. Due to the subject matter of the film, it was predominately an African-American audience. And, because of the great soundtrack for the film, created by Curtis Mayfield, people were dancing in the aisles.

It was a great experience. I sat there alone, as none of my friends wanted to go and see the film with me, just melting into the whole experience.

I saw that movie several times at that theater and at other places. It was a big influence on my filmmaking ideology that came into play many years later. It's still a great movie to watch. In fact, this was one of the two films that truly influenced my eventual cinematic expression, the other was *Easy Rider*.

Certainly, this was not a high-budget film. What it did was to truly utilize the landscape of New York City, in the winter, to the advantage of its whole cinematic expression. This film, and movies like this, really taught me, as a filmmaker, to set your storylines and to film in locations that really allow you to take advantage of the beauty of disintegrating urban landscapes.

One of things that struck me last night, while watching the film… Well, I guess it is simply something that I was caused to rethink, was that in the physical combat scenes in the movie, several of the punches and kicks don't really connect. This is something that is so common of quickly-made films of that era. Even in martial art orientated films like *Black Belt Jones,* which starred Jim Kelly, who first came to film notoriety in the greatest martial art film ever made, *Enter the Dragon*, sometimes the fight choreography just doesn't work. This is something that I came to realized very early on in my filmmaking career, unless you have the time and the budget to truly take the time to get the choreography down to perfection, it's not going to look all that good if you run techniques together as there will be mistakes and, for lack of a better term, cheesy fight moves.

Mind you, at least as far as I am concerned, this does not take away from the film. In fact, as a filmmaker, it allows me to be focused into witnessing the cinematic process. But, the thing that it did cause me to think about last night is, say if one of my films were to have that level of fight inaccurate in the fight choreography, the critics would tear it apart. I mean, there are all of these internet-based critics out there now, talking about whatever it is they talk about, but they have never made a movie with fight scenes, so they don't know how hard it is to truly get every technique to sell. That's why, (and here's a cinematic secret for you), long ago I discovered that you shoot one technique at a time, move the camera, and then shoot the next. With this, you can at least control each movement and hopefully make it sell. But, I never heard one critic bagging on the fighting in Super Fly because back then people were looking to the overall vision of a film and the filmmaker and they were not only looking to find fault.

In life, I think this is an important mindset to keep in mind and to question of yourself, what are you focusing on viewing? Are you looking for fault? Or, are you looking for the art in each subject matter and each person that is laid out in front of you?

Kind of a funny sidebar here… I was doing the family dinner thing, on Christmas, over at the cousin of my lady's house. He and his wife hold it there most of the time and you can tell that he, the husband, really lays out the spread, he really takes the time and cares enough to try to do things right. It's art! I really appreciate that level of effort.

Anyway… We got on the subject and I made the joke (kinda) to his wife about the family talking trash about my lady and me when we weren't around. For those of you who don't know, that just seems to be what people of Korean heritage do, find a target and attack when they're not around. Me, I'm an easy target. *"Were your ears burning,"* she jokingly questioned. …You know, that old saying, when someone is speaking about you and you're not around, your ears burn. Confirming that is what they do.

My point is, and this is what I take throughout my life, you can look for the fault in anything and/or anybody if that is what you want to do. But, in doing that, you lose the grace of all of the art that exists in anyone's anything. Sure, you can see that maybe the fight scenes in *Super Fly* weren't that perfectly choreographed. But, if you focus on that, you miss the perfection of the cinematic art that is presented in that movie.

You have to ask yourself, are you an artist or are you a critic? Critics unleash the hate, seeking out any fault that can find, even if that fault is only conjured up in their own mind. That is just what they do. But, does hate ever equal anything good? Does finding fault ever make anything any better?

On the other hand, if you allow yourself to see the beauty in all things. If you allow yourself to witness the art that is, even if that art does not live up to all of your expectations, then what arises is the ability to find perfection and even satori it all that you witness.

Think about this the next time you are looking for fault, about to find fault, and are about to express the fault you believe you have found in anyone or anything. My opinion, find beauty in fault, then true art reigns supreme.

Who Are You Going to Help Today?
27/Dec/2022 08:20 AM

Who are you going to help today?

What good are you going to do today?

When most people think about helping someone, they define that help by what they believe that someone else need. They define that help by them giving that someone what they want to give them. But, is that help or is that simply you projecting what you think a person needs onto that individual?

Throughout history and throughout time we have all encountered and heard the stories of people doing for other people—believing they knew what was best for that person. For most of us, when we were young, our parents did things for us. The problem was, in many cases, what they did was simply them attempting to force their morals, their ideas, and their life rules onto us. Though those ideologies may have worked for them, they did not work for or define the time and the place where we lived. Thus, though they believed they were helping, they were not.

As we got older, for most, there have certainly been times when someone did something for us, like telling their lover, *"I'm no good for you. Forget about me."* When that was not at all what the other person wanted to hear. The one person may have falsely believed they were helping, and maybe in their mind they were, but, in fact, all they were doing was projecting their mindset of their specific desires onto that other individual.

Of course, the list goes on and on from there; one person telling themselves that they are helping someone, when all they are doing is giving a person what they want to give or projecting their fantasy of reality onto that other person.

Think about your own life. Who have you helped? Was the help you gave them the help they wanted or was they help you gave them what you thought they needed?

Think about your own life. Have you been asked to help someone, but what they asked you to do to help them, hurt someone else. Was that truly helping or was that hurting? Because if you hurt one person by believing you are helping another, who's going to get hit with the karma?

Help is a complicated subject. Yes, we should all help all those that we can help. But, if you are helping simply based in your need to project your own reality onto that someone else or giving them what you believe they need, that is not help, that is just projected dominance.

Who are you going to help today?

What good are you going to do today?

Putting the Band Back Together
26/Dec/2022 02:32 PM

For any filmmaker they understand that one of the most essential elements of any cinematic project is the cast. …Well, I guess that's only true if you are making a story-driven, narrative feature film. But, as this is the foundation of most movies, the cast is at least one of the most primary components.

For someone like me, who has made a lot of films, I have met and worked with a lot of actors and actresses. With very few exceptions, they have all been great and talented people. The thing about the film games is, however, people move along, you lose track. Unless you become friends, it is not uncommon that you fall out of contact with someone. Even if you do become friends, sometimes people move away from your life. This is not to say that you did not appreciate their presence when you were working them. But, the reality of the reality is, sometimes you lose touch. Certainly, this has been the case with me with many of the people who have appeared in my films.

About fifteen years ago, I fully shifted away from doing story-driven films; delving wholly into what I call, *The Non-Narrative Zen Film*. Meaning, I no longer was creating my film ventures around actor-orientated projects. Though there was a lot of reasons for this, mostly it just seemed that it was my destiny to explore the more abstract realms of filmmaking.

This being said, it has forever been the case that it is the viewers, and the journalists, and the critics, and the film historians that have primarily forced their attention on discussing my narrative pieces—at least so far. Hand-in-hand with this fact, I frequently am contacted by people who throw their hat into the acting ring and would like to be in one of my Zen Films. Many of these people bring up movies like, *The Roller Blade Seven,* and question if I would ever be willing to do another picture like that as that film has become somewhat of a pinnacle in the Annals of Cult Filmmaking history? As stated so many times, *"Of course I would."* The thing is, and something that the non-filmmakers out there commonly overlooks, a film like that took a lot of time to create.

I've discussed RB7 so many times in so many places. And, like I've said many times before, the cast really helped to make that film what it became. ...The number of cast members really added to the overall depth of that movie; the first Zen Film.

What those two statements mean is that, it would be very hard to do a film like that today, without a lot of money. And, money is the one element that few people can bring to the table. You just couldn't go out there and do today what we did back then without renting large locations and paying a large cast and crew. The fact is, it was a different time and people possessed a different mindset when we created RB7. It wasn't just about getting paid, it was about being a part of a film and becoming a participant of cinematic art.

I am often cofounded by the people who have never lived or worked here in Hollywood. Those who throw all of their judgmental criticism in the direction of that film and films like that. They weren't here! They weren't a part of that production and most likely never were a part of any other Hollywood No-Budget, Indie Production, so they just don't get it!

But, before I get too far off track… It would be hard to do today what we, just two people, Donald G. Jackson and myself, put together back then. But, this is not to say that it wouldn't be nice to try!

As time has progressed, and my filmmaking sense, in association with actors and actresses improved, I got the indie shoot down to a science. It doesn't have to take a lot of time to create a feature film. I got it to the point where I would bring in a cast member and in a few hours I would have their scenes all shot. You can read all about my two-day movie theory in my book, *Independent Filmmaking: Secrets of the Craft,* if you feel like it.

The point being, the actors I have worked with have each made my films what they are and I thank and appreciate all of them. But, times move on and you lose track…

For a long time now, (years really), especially when one of these actors or actresses contacts me, like a couple did during this holiday season, I think that we, they and I, and all of those from the larger Zen Film talent pool, should all get back together and make another movie together. …Get together all of those actors and actresses that were in a Scott Shaw Zen Film and do another one. Maybe even one as grand as RB7 or at least *Samurai Vampire Bikers from Hell.* We can even bring in some of you new people who want to check out the magic of *Zen Filmmaking,* as well.

I understand some of my close *Zen Filmmaking* sisters and brothers have passed away and left this earth. That's truly sad! Others, most of us, have gotten older. We don't look the way we used to appear. But, that doesn't mean there is no reason that we shouldn't be on-screen together again.

The fact is, it has been me who shifted his focus away from cast members. That's my fault. But, that doesn't mean that we shouldn't get the band back together. You know, like they did in the movie, *The Blues Brothers… "We're on a mission from god,"* and all that.

I don't know??? Maybe you can't go back??? Maybe I've just thinking of times gone past??? But, if you're out there and reading this, and have a place for us to shoot or something like that, give me a shout, maybe we can make another Zen Film.

Forgiving Those Who Won't Forgive
25/Dec/2022 07:18 AM

In all chosen relationships, it involves two or more people choosing to be together. There are all of those relationships that we do not choose: family, workplace, and the like. But, for those we do choose, it is a choice we make to come together.

The thing that ends most relationships is that someone does something that the other participant does not like. But, here's the thing, if you care about that person, if you want to stay in a relationship with that person, when they do that something that you do not like, yes, you may get mad at them for doing it, but that anger will pass, and you forgive them. What causes a relationship to end? Someone who will not forgive.

I was at this temple yesterday. There was a statue of their main guru. Underneath it there was, (I guess), his main saying, *"Love everyone, trust few."* Wow, I thought, that was pretty strange. You would think that a true teacher's teaching would be much more pure, profound, and more positive than that. Like my teacher, Swami Satchidananda's main saying was, *"Truth is one, paths are many."* And, it seems all the other gurus say what they say with so much more positivity. So???

Reflecting on that saying, it made my lady and I go into some joking rhetoric. I said, *"Love hot young women who want to have sex with you, trust no one."* Yes, yes, I know some of you may take offense at that statement. It's misogynistic. But, if you can't have a little fun in life and be politically incorrect every now and then, what's the point of existence? And yeah, isn't it great when someone just desires you to desire you and/or loves you to love you? Plus, at least from my life experience(s) the, *"Trust no one,"* part is true.

But, all this comes down to the point and the purpose of life. We choose to be with someone for whatever reason, but how many of those people that you once chose to be with are you still with? If you're with a lot of them, good for you. If this is the case, obviously, when they did something wrong, you forgave them. But, here's the catch; when they did something wrong to you, was what they did right for them? You see, this is where the whole complication of life and life-relationships comes into play. What is right for them may not be right for you. Just as what is right for you may not be right for them.

Here lies the source point for all relationships. Are you willing to let the individual you are in that relationship with do what is right for them even if it is wrong for you? Can you forgive them for they being who they are? Can they forgive you for you being who you are? But, even more importantly, are they/are you evolved enough to care enough about that other person to not do what will cause them discomfort in the first place—just because you/they want to do something?

Who do you forgive? Why do you forgive them?

Who will you not forgive? Why will you not forgive them?

Who forgives you? Why did they forgive you?

Who will not forgive you? Why will they not forgive you?

And, are willing to do nothing that will require forgiveness in the future?

* * *
23/Dec/2022 07:14 AM

If you've hurt one person you've hurt everyone.

* * *
23/Dec/2022 07:13 AM

Whatever it is you do, what you do should make people feel better by your doing it.

* * *
23/Dec/2022 07:13 AM

What happens if there is no hell?

* * *
23/Dec/2022 07:12 AM

The next time you say something negative about someone say something more negative about yourself.

* * *
22/Dec/2022 07:48 AM

If you don't start you can never finish.

The Influence of Taoism on Traditional Chinese Art
22/Dec/2022 07:15 AM

For anyone who's ever been in Grad School you know you've got to write a lot of papers. I was just going through the collections of papers I wrote during one of my stints and I came upon this study I put together for one of my classes. Thought it was kinda interesting. So, here it is for you to read if you feel like it.

The Influence of Taoism on Traditional Chinese Art
Scott Shaw

Taoism is a mystical school of thought. As such, the influence it has had upon the various factors of Chinese culture, including that of the arts, has been brought about by individuals who have practiced Taoist thinking and expounding their understanding by various methods, including: painting, poetry, and music.

Taoism can be broken up into three primary secular schools of thought. As such, there is not one school of Taoist thinking which can be delineated as having the sole influence over defining the Taoist arts of China. There is the rational school of Taoism, being very pragmatic in nature; the Confucian school of Taoism, which honored the State and set about defining its practices as dominated by an obedience to the Dynasty and to a lesser degree honoring the omnipresent, supernatural Tao; and finally, there is the mystical school of Taoism, defined by the works of Lao Tzu and Chuang Tzu. In the definitive text of this school, Tao Te Ching, it states,

"The great Tao flows everywhere, both to the left and to the right. The ten thousand things depend upon it; it holds nothing back. It fulfills its purposes silently and makes no claim. It nourishes the ten thousand things."

The, Tao Te Ching, goes on to state, *"Practice non action. Work without doing."*

Therefore, to a practitioner of this school of Taoist thought, an individual should not, in fact, create works of art at all, as all unnecessary action ultimately separates one from the Tao. One should, instead, abide solely by the laws of nature.

The mystic school of Taoists thought, though not intended by its founders to form creative works, has, none-the-less, been the primary source of influence on the Taoist arts of China. The mystical school possess a reverence for nature, lacking in the other two previously stated Taoist ideologies. To this end, nature is commonly depicted in creative works by practitioners of this thought process.

To begin this study, we can view two of the paintings created in the Northern Sung Dynasty. The Sung Dynasty existed between 960 and 1279 AD. This is considered one of the high points of China's artistic history. This is because of the fact that due to bureaucratic centralization and economic regulation the Chinese society, on the whole, flourished.

During the Sung Dynasty, landscape painting rose to a new level of perfection. As interaction with nature is a central theme to mystical Taoism, we can initially see how this philosophy directly influenced the paintings of the time.

The first painting is a landscape painted by, Li T'ang, sometime during the early twelfth century. (See Illustration 1). The viewer, when viewing this painting, initially sees that the landscape is composed of steep mountains in the background, with the foreground filled with trees and a stream. These images were common to the eyes of those who lived in this region of China. Thus, they were not created from imagination or memory. Instead, it was the artist's attempt to form an illustrative depiction of the closeness he encountered with nature and Tao while painting it.

When viewing a Chinese painting which possess the influence of mystical Taoism, as do Sung Period landscapes, one must understand the interrelationship between void and solid. To the Western artist, all space must be filled with image or color, in order for the painting to achieve ultimate purpose. To the Taoist influenced Chinese painter, on the other hand, void or unpainted space is as equally important as filled zones on the painting. As is stated in the Tao Te Ching,

"Shape clay into a vessel; It is the space within that makes it useful. Cut doors and windows for a room; It is the holes which make it useful."

In the case of this painting, the background mountains are not highly detailed. From this, the viewer is drawn to witness them and move into the void they possess. Thus, moving in towards the omnipresence of Tao.

George Rowley, in his book, Principles of Chinese Painting, states,

"In China sensuous effects were conditioned by obedience to natural principles and were limited to the 'essence of the idea.'"

With this ideology one can immediately see that the Taoist artist searched deeply into the soul of the objects they painted in order to bring the individual who viewed the work closer to the essence of Tao which exists in nature. This was often times most precisely brought about by not attempting to plainly detail images they could not perfectly illustrate.

In a second painting from this period, the work of Li Kung-nien, (see illustration 2), again the viewer witnesses a similar image with the foreground detailed and the background left to the abstract

Rowley states, *"They, (the Chinese), practiced the principle of the moving focus, by which the eye could wander while the spectator also wandered in imagination through the landscape."*

When viewing this painting one could become lost in the intricacies of the foreground trees, as the darkness draws one's eyes to them. Equally, with the subtle outlining of the mountains, in dark coloring, one is propelled up to their vastness as one would be drawn to the Tao.

By viewing two paintings from relatively the same time period, but linked to the Southern Sung Dynasty; namely, *"Water Fall,"* by an anonymous artist and *"Village of Clearing Mist,"* by Ying Yu-chien, (see illustrations 3 and 4), one immediately sees that they do not depict steep mountain regions, as do the two previous. This fact is obviously due to geographic influences. They both do, however, illustrate nature.

As union with nature is the encompassing element of mystical Taoism, all of the physical creations liked to Taoism possess nature's essence. Rowley states, in his discussion of this,

"By the single daring assumption of the cosmic principle of the Tao, the Chinese focused on the notion of one power permeating the whole universe, instead of emphasizing the Western dualism of spirit and matter, creator and created, animate and inanimate, and human and nonhuman. This concept of the Tao was the touchstone of Chinese painting which affected the creative imagination, the subject matter and the interpretations. Although it originated in the musings about the cosmos, it became reworked by the Sung painters into the living reality' which they sought to paint."

The *"Waterfall"* painting is very abstract in its illustration. This allows the viewer to dwell on the continuous flow of energy throughout nature, obviously linking one to Tao. The *"Village of Clearing Mist,"* painting is equally abstract, drawing the viewer to seek deeply into its lined images where the village begins, and how it merges into the surrounding landscape.

Mystical Taoism is perhaps most precisely depicted with paintings. For in these works, the viewer is allowed to seek the image at the source of the lines and ultimately be directed to the merging of image with Tao. There is, however, other art forms which have been influenced by Taoism in China, among them, poetry.

There are six principals of Chinese poetry; they are: *'Feng'* the customs or manner of a particular district as a subject or verse, *'Ya'* and *'Sung'* which refers to all kinds of royal court events, *'Pi'* is metaphor, *'Fu'* is the simple narration of events, and *'hsing'* is the focus on nature. Though each of these factors play a part in various forms of Chinese poetry there is no cohesive union of form or overall strategy to using them in the actual writing of Chinese poetry.

Chinese Taoist influenced poetry varies. It does not possess a formalized format. Though during certain periods, a similar structure can be found, there has never been a universal formula. For this reason, most of the assertions of scholars of Chinese poetry are speculations and attempted formulas, based more on the Chinese linguists than in the facts of Taoism influencing a given poem or poetic group. For example, James J.Y. Liu, attempts to define elements of the Chinese language in his book, The Art of Chinese Poetry,

"As Chinese does not require any indication of 'number,' the poet need not bother about such irrelevant details and can concentrate on his main task of presenting the spirit of a tranquil spring night among the mountains. Moreover, the absence of 'tense' in Chinese enables the poet to present the scene not from the point of view of any specific time..."

Though in essence what he is saying is true, what he fails to explain is the fact that in the Chinese language, though number and tense need not be present in a statement, the word itself will change when different numbers or tenses are discussed.

What Liu has done in his book is to go through and rationalize Chinese poetry from an academic standpoint, depicting meter, time, syllabic value, and so on. Chinese poetry, however, does not possess the exacting quality of Japanese Haiku. There is especially no standard formalized tradition of poetry relating to the school of Taoism in China, as Haiku is a depiction of Zen. Therefore, though he appears to reach valid conclusions, what he says is based more in his study of Chinese language then that of a reference to actual Chinese cultural influences, especially Taoism.

If we think in terms of Taoist understanding, what occurs when one studies Chinese poetry is, one witnesses an attempt by an individual to give form to the formless. Which is, in fact, in direct contradiction to Taoist thinking. Various types of Chinese poetry can be detailed as having been created at a given period of time or by a specific poetic group who practiced a prescribed type of thought. In either case, it is simply an attempt to formulate rules of poetry dictated by what has previously occurred, not necessarily by what was in the minds of the individuals who created the poetry.

If we view two poems created at different periods of Chinese history, we can see how little they influence one another and, in fact, how little influence Taoism has on the overall poetry of China. In the poem written by Wang, An-shih (1021-1086), he states,

"A stone bridge spans the vast void, A thatched hut overlooks the clear water. Bending to peep at the delicate almond blooms, I feel the image is as good as the original: Charming the Lady of the Ching-yang Palace Who, smiling, leapt into the well. Sad it is to see the tiny ripples Spoil her fading make-up beyond repair."

Here we see a classic case of a man, who obviously admires a woman, while depicting what happens to her. This poem is not more abstract than one written by a modern poet. It does not reflect any actions of spiritual or Taoist essence. Therefore, it proves the point that Chinese poetry is not universally dominated by a spiritual dimension.

In the case of the more spiritually orientated poet such as, Wang Wei, we can see by studying one of his poems, that due to his mind set in the abstract spirituality of Ch'an (Chinese Zen Buddhism), he depicts a scene which is much more abstract and less focalized on his actual desires or preference.

"Moon rise surprise mountain bird. Occasionally cry in spring valley"

By viewing the previous two poems, one can immediately understand the mindset of the poet. When spirituality is referenced, in Chinese, it is obvious. If it is there, it is there. If it is not, it is not.

Early Chinese artists were driven to depict the spiritual images they encountered and relay them to the surrounding world. The Chinese poet, on the other hand, is not so determined.

When one listens to traditional Chinese music, played upon a Ch'in, one immediately can hear the lack of obvious imposed structure which exists within Western music. The noting which takes place, may well be defined and orchestrated, yet its structure appears to be much more freeform, as its tempo moves without apparent bonding to a precise scale or timing.

The music the Ch'in produces is simple, much more simple than that of a guitar or violin, Western stringed instrument. With Western instruments, the musical patterns and their structure tend to be full of sound. In the case of the Ch'in there is noticeable time between each note, allowing the listener to experience the space in between the notes very clearly.

From the Ch'in the simplicity and embodiment of Tao is embraced. This is due to the fact that evident structure is absent, and the listener is drawn into a space of meditative awareness.

Bibliography

Aria, Barbara and Gon, Russell Eng, *"The Spirit of the Chinese Character."* San Fransisco, 1992, Chronicle Books.

Cottrell, Arthur and Morgan, David, *"China's Civilization: A Survey of it's History, Arts, and Technology."* New York, 1975, Preger Publishers.

Dawson, Raymond, *"Imperial China."* London, 1972, Hutchisons of London.

Fairbanks, John K. and Reischaver, *"China."* Boston, 1989, Houghton Muffin, Company.

Feng, Gia-fu and English, Jane, Trans. *"Chuang Tsu: Inner Chapters."* New York, 1974, Vintage Books.

Feng, Gia-fu and English, Jane, Trans. *"Tao Te Ching."* New York, 1972, Vintage Books.

Giles, Herbert A., *"The Civilization of China."* New York, 1911, Henry Holt and Company.

Girardut, N.J., *"Myth and Meaning in Early Taoism: The Theme of Chaos."* Berkeley, 1983, University of California Press.

Graham, A.C., *"Disputers of Tao."* La Salle, 1989, Open Court. Latourette,
Kenneth Scott, *"The Chinese: Their History and Culture."* New York, 1962, The MacMillan Company.

Legge, James. *"Confucius: Confucian Analects, The Great Learning, The Doctrines of the Mean."* New York, 1971 Dover Publications.

Legge, James. *"The Four Books."* Taipei, 1891 Li Fuk Publications.

Liu, Da, *"The Tao of Chinese Culture."* New York, 1979, Schocker Books.

Liu, James J.Y. *"The Art of Chinese Poetry."* Chicago, 1962, University of Chicago Press.

Rowley, George, *"Principals of Chinese Painting."* 1947, Princeton, Princeton University Press.

Keith, Ilza, *"The Yellow's Emperor's Classic of Internal Medicine."* Berkeley, 1949 University of California Press.

Watts, Alan, *"Tao: The Watercourse Way."* New York, 1975, Pantheon Books.

Welch, Holmes, *"The Parting of the Way: Lao Tsu and the Taoist Movement."* Boston, 1957, Beacon Press.

Wu, John C.H., *"The Golden Age of Zen."* New York, 1996, Image Books.

Yang, C,K., *"Religion in Chinese Society."* Berkeley, 1970, University of California Press.

Somebody's Biography but Not Mine
21/Dec/2022 05:06 PM

More out of necessity than desire, I've been forced to come up with a few catch phrases that describe my reality in the world. A couple of my main ones are, *"You know you're famous when people you've never met say things about you that aren't true."* And, *"They're the ones talking about me, I'm not the one talking about them."*

The first one came to me as I was walking into the NAMM Show many years ago. That's a show that happens twice a year: one here in SoCal and the other in Nashville. It's a place where all the musical equipment manufactures show their wares. A lot of rock stars walk the floors, a lot of has-beens, (at least they once were), and a lot of wanta-bes. Or, as my lady likes to describe it, *"A bunch of ugly old white guys with long hair."*

It's kind of hard to get a pass to get in. You can't just show up. But, all that's for them to explain.

Anyway… As I was walking in that day, I was walking next to a guy who had become the singer for a superstar band from the 80s, after their original singer had taken his own life. He competed and won the gig via one of those broadcast TV shows, so he had a lot of instant fame.

As I walked near to him, I could see he was rockin' all of this arrogance and ego. I could also hear a couple of people saying things like, *"That's, that guy."* He also got a few sneers. Interesting, I thought. He won his way to the top and instantly he was both loved and hated but no one really knew anything about him.

Soon after this, however, he detailed on MySpace, (this was back in the days when MySpace was THE social media platform), that he was on his way back to Canada as the gig didn't work out. I felt a bit sorry for him.

Me, at that exact point in time, I was thinking about this piece that had just come out about me, published on a martial arts website. It had been written by this university employed Ph.D. The article was set up with references, and stuff, just like an academic paper. I remember thinking that I just couldn't believe that anyone would waste their time doing something like that about me. I mean, it was just your basic smear editorial made up to look like something more. I remember thinking and stating, *"This is so National Enquirer."* This was long before TMZ.

Personally, I find all of that kind of stuff fairly amusing. That's just who I am. I can easily poke fun at myself. Though, in truth, that kind of doing does breeds negativity. And, when you're on the receiving end of that, it ain't fun.

I know I've said this before, but via these types of things, I've gotten a few death threats. Those always strike me in this weird place. I mean, why would someone threaten to kill me just because of what someone else has said? They don't know me. I never did anything to them. Yet, just because someone said something about me, that is based in a lie or a brutal critique of my life or my creations, someone threatens to kill me. How wrong is that?

Speaking of TMZ… I was flipping channels maybe a week or so ago and Charles on TMZ said, *"Pretty much everyone famous gets those, (death threats)."* But, I'm not famous. Plus, I'm a guy who bases his whole life around positivity and helping (or at least attempting) to help others. Kill me??? For what??? I just don't get it???

Which kind of brings me to the point of all this. Again, this afternoon, I got forwarded a piece detailing the supposed who, what, when, where, and why of my relationship with Donald G. Jackson. The thing is, it was one-hundred precent wrong. Everything that person wrote was incorrect. But, there they were, someone saying it like it was some kind of fact. There were others believing what that person said and commenting on it. But, if the inception of anything is based in false-facts, everything after that is completely erroneous. Plus, it looks like this individual has written all kinds of negative stuff about me and my films. Why??? They obviously don't know me.

I don't know... Maybe I should start calling these people out, pointing a finger at them, naming names, and telling the world how they don't check their facts and are making a bunch of false, misleading, or biased proclamations based upon nothing more than what's going on in their own brain. But then, you place all the false statements that are made about me and my films, based upon some erroneous something that someone heard from someone else, that would become a full-time job. I mean, People, talk about your own shit instead of speaking about someone else's!

I have written so much stuff, and it's all on this website for FREE. I've written about my life, my filmmaking, my career, my reasons for why I do what I do, my working with Donald G. Jackson: how we met, why we worked together, what we created, and what occurred after his death. I mean, this person didn't even know that Don has been dead for almost twenty years. Yet, he is propagating his truth, which are just lies, to the world. Like Jimmy on South Park says, *"I mean, come on..."*

I always question, why do people focus on the life and the creative works of others? Don't they have anything better to do? Maybe, go make your own movie, so people can criticize it. But, more than that, why do people seek to evoke, incite, and castigate a person for being who they are and particularly for an artist presenting the world with their vision of art? Isn't art one of the highest forms of human evolution?

You know, there's a lot a people making money by critiquing movies and stuff like that on-line. There's a lot of people who watch their presentations. One of things that I always find amusing is that there are more people who have watched people dissertating about my movies than have actually watched my Zen Films on places like YouTube and stuff. Wouldn't you rather form your own ideas rather than listen to those presented by someone else—someone who is wrong in what they are saying?

I guess you have to be on my side of the arena to truly understand what I feel. But, I am certain that we all have encountered life situations where people think they know us or they believe they understand something about us, but they are completely wrong. Shouldn't that be motivation enough not to fall prey to the untruthful words of others? Shouldn't that cause us ALL to only seek our own truth?

In closing, I guess let me say one more time, *"You know you're famous when people you've never met say things about you that aren't true."* Awh, what the hell… I guess it gives me something to write about; right?

Here's an idea, you should make up your own saying to describe the life you live. Think about it. Have some fun with it. You never know, it may open up an entirely new realm of life understanding for you.

* * *
21/Dec/2022 06:59 AM

Is superstition religion?

Is religion superstition?

Jōdo Shinshū
20/Dec/2022 07:31 AM

  Jōdo Shinshū or True Pure Land Buddhism or Shin Buddhism rose to become a highly practiced form of Buddhist teaching during the early Kamakura Period of Japan's history. Though it has declined and risen in prominence in Japan and the world since its inception, it is still a highly practiced school of Mahayana Buddhism.
  Perhaps one of the most important beliefs propagated by this system is that it was taught that we, humanity, is in a state of spiritual decline and those seeking enlightenment are only doing so as a pursue based in ego.
  If we take a moment to look at this concept, we first understand that how many people are actually seeking enlightenment? Answer: Very few. Are you? Most people never even contemplate the pathway to achieving this ultimate state of human existence. With this simple understanding as a basis, we can easily conclude that the founder of this system, Shinran, and its other proponents were correct in their statement.
  Moreover, for those who do follow the path towards obtaining nirvana, why are they doing it? For most, it is a quest, which by its very nature is something based in ego and, thus, is against the true teachings of the Buddha.
  If we look at this entire system of teaching a bit deeper, we realize that it was created a century ago. If the mind of humanity was thought to be in decline at that point in time, has anything gotten any better?
  There is a caveat to all of this, however. Like so many other beliefs and teachings, religions in particular, people have the tendency to look to the past and cast their idea that, *"Then,"* was a more spiritual time. But, was it? Were the people truly any different? Yes, times and cultures and political definitions and technology has changed, but have people truly changed? My guess is that they have not. Were

they truly more spiritual back then? Maybe more superstitious, but I doubt more truly spiritual.

What then are we left with? We are left with what we are left with. We are left with what we have right not. We are left with who we are, as a world society, at this point in history.

Here, it comes down to you. What are you going to do with that fact? What are you going to do with your life? Are you going to follow a path of ego-driven acquisition or are you going to follow the road to enlightenment? At the end of your days, which one do you believe will have provided you with the best True Life that you could have lived?

*   *   *
20/Dec/2022 06:49 AM

Everybody wants to commit the sins, but no one wants to pay for their sins.

The Artist and Their Paintbrush, the Filmmaker and Their Camera
19/Dec/2022 07:44 AM

When one thinks of art, the first thought for many that comes to mind is the image of a person standing in front of a canvas with a paintbrush. It is just them and their art. On that canvas, they are attempting to bring what they envision in their mind and portray it upon that canvas. Though this may be the most idealized image of an artist at work, we all certainly understand that art transcended beyond the canvas and onto many other levels of creation.

Without getting too esoteric here, art can loosely be defined as someone creating something. That, *"Something,"* can be found in so many varying forms. And, through time, that, *"Created Something,"* has continued to expand as technology has continued to evolve.

For many, they lock their mind into what they believe art to be. For most, they like what they like and do not like what they do not like. If they do not like what they are looking at, if they do not like whatever it was that was created, all they can exclaim is, *"That's not art!"* But, no matter what anyone says, True Art is defined solely in the mind of the creator.

Having personally walked the path of creating many forms of what I consider art throughout my lifetime, I understand the feeling of finding a medium and then finding a way to follow through and bring what I see in my mind into physical reality. Has everyone liked the ART I have created? No, of course not. But, isn't that the true definition of art, creating something that causes the viewer to think and to feel?

From the moment I seriously got into filmmaking, as a transition and expansion from photography, I would often find my bliss in going out solo with just a film camera and filming moving images. Many of these moving images found their way into my creations. Though, in my early years, I attempted to follow the more traditional path of a story and character-driven production, there were always those elements of my filming images, all by myself, that would find their way into my cinematic creations.

Maybe twenty years ago or so, I begin to realize that, all least in my definition of my cinematic art, the storyline and the characters needed to be dropped all together, leaving only the moving images as the expression of my filmmaking art. I called it, *the Non-Narrative, Zen Film,* but it could be called anything, as I am certainly not the first filmmaker to produce films such as this.

As time moved on, this became my primary focus of filmmaking. Why? Because for me, it is the pure exhibiting of cinematic art, leading to cinematic enlightenment. It does not require the participation of actors or crewmember. All that is required is the artist and his tool, namely his camera. At least for me, this removes many of the unnecessary elements and guides a cinematic creation towards it most pure and most, *"Zen,"* form; just the artist and their canvas.

If you create, try it. Try removing all of the unnecessary elements from your art. You never know, you may find a new space of creating the perfect expression of art.

* * *
17/Dec/2022 11:36 AM

Those who are not an artist can only criticize art.

At a Certain Point Your Style Doesn't Matter
16/Dec/2022 09:58 AM

This is a piece directed primarily towards the martial artists out there.

As someone who has actively practiced the martial arts for just under sixty years, I believe I possess a fairly good understanding of how one evolves as a practitioner of these forms of self-defense. When one begins their practice, it is often the case that they become very protective of their teacher, their school, and their style. This is especially the case if they have truly taken to the system they are training in and the instructor or instructors who are teaching them in their art are proving them with useful techniques in an agreeable manner.

The fact is, there are some instructors who are just not very good. Maybe they are rude, maybe they are egocentric, maybe they are money-hungry forcing students to sign long-term contracts, maybe they are demeaning to their students, or, like in the case of one of my instructors when I was an adolescent, they single out one of their students and continually use them for their demonstration dummy. With this, a student may either lose interest in the martial arts all together or change schools, if not styles.

The focus of this piece is not on the bad instructors, however. It is about the ones who truly provide a lifelong service to their students, teaching them viable techniques based in a specific style orientated syllabus. For those students—those who stay long-term, earning their black belt, and those who possibly become instructors, they are the ones who may become very style-centric.

If we look to history, prior to the twentieth century, very few martial artists moved between systems. This was not only based in a local and cultural programing, but it was also based in available. Generally, there were few choices among schools of martial arts in a specific community.

Moreover, and the fact being, very few people chose to follow the path of the martial arts.

It must be noted, that among most Asian societies, a person who practiced the martial arts was actually looked down upon by general society as they were thought to be one who was conscribed to a lower class, a lessor mindset, and/or someone who followed the barbaric practices of physical combat. Though modern media has all but erased this fact from modern knowledge, and has idealized and glorified the martial artist, this was not, in fact, the case throughout most of world history.

As the twentieth century came upon us, and international cultural interaction became more frequent, the martial arts found their way to the West. From this, the early Western practitioner attempted to culturally emulate the mind, words, and techniques of their Asian instructors, mostly with less-than-ideal impersonations. They attempted to mimic instead of emulate. Thus, even though many of these first-generation Western instructors held fast to their systems, what they understood and what they actually taught was lacking a true sense of source knowledge.

In fact, to this day, this mindset has not changed very much. There are many Western instructor, claiming advanced knowledge of a style, but not speaking the language of where the system originated while attempting to produce the words used in the dissemination of the system poorly, and, form this, missing some of the elemental knowledge that can and could only be had by possessing a true linguist and cultural understanding of what they are claiming to teach. Many, if not most, of these instructors have not even traveled to and/or studied their system of self-defense in the land where it was originated.

During the twentieth century there came to be more and more Asian and Western instructors teaching the martial arts in the Western world. From this, there began to be the ability for a practitioner to view the various styles of self-defense that were now congregated in one location that had originally hailed from all across the globe. Because of this fact, some practitioners began to integrate and adapt techniques from the various system into their own singular practice. Some of the most notable people who first did this were Chuck Norris and a bit later Bruce Lee. Both of these individuals achieved great fame. But, there were also many other practitioners, who employed this method of integration, who no one ever heard as they began the process of incorporating the various styles of martial arts into one conglomerative system of self-defense in their small schools or backyards.

Though there were, and still are, many who believe this practice is a bastardization of the martial arts, in many ways it has freed the practitioner from being locked into only one, very stylized, system, thereby allowing them to integrate and combine the techniques from various styles into a conglomeration that becomes more effective for not only they, themselves, but for their students, as well. From this, the need to poorly imitate one culture has been bypassed. Emerging is an all-encompassing non-style of a style that is allowed to continually evolve as new understandings are developed.

As martial artists we can learn from this integration and as human beings we can also gain from this understanding. By opening our minds to new ideas, and not being forcefully locked into a tradition that may never be truly understood, we allow ourselves to be the vessel where all knowledge may be studied, acquired, and ultimately understood in a freeform mindset not limited by dogma.

Takin' It to the Streets
15/Dec/2022 08:47 AM

I always find it rather interesting how people focus on the goings-on of other people. How they become so enthralled with the lives of others, particularly when something negative is going on in that other person's life. I mean, earlier this year, it was all about the Johnny and Amber trial and now it's all about Harry and Megan. WHY??? Why do people need some reason to focus outside of themselves? Why are they more worried about the With-Out as opposed to the With-In?

Well, I guess that's only partially true. Think about a time when you were really upset with someone. Then/there you were all about living your moment. But, then that moment passed and then what?

From what I hear, it seems like Harry and his family, due, in no small part to his relationship with Megan, had some big row. This is apparently all disseminated in the new addition to the Netflix series about them that came out today.

Now, let me preface this by saying, I could care less about that series. I could care less about Harry and Megan. But, as it is all over the news services, I have heard and seen little tidbits of it. Just like I said about the Johnny and Amber trial, it's none of my business, so why should I care? Yet, everybody does seem to care. They want to poke their nose in other people's business. Business that is none of their business.

I mean, look around you, how many people are enthralled with all of this? And, it's not just Harry and Megan or Johnny and Amber or Megan Thee Stallion and Tory Lanez or whatever else is going on in whomever else's life, at whatever moment in time, people are transfixed. Just look on the internet, how many people are discussing the life of others verses how many people are trying to rise their own level of consciousness in order to make themselves a better and more whole and enlightened individual? Everybody thinks and talks about everybody else. But, why?

The answer to that is easy. The answer is, it is easy. If you focus outside of yourself, you don't have to look within. If you focus outside of yourself and shift the conversation to speaking about other people, no one will be thinking about and discussing your flaws.

This being said, does that make it right? Does taking the drug of thinking about and discussing someone else really make your life any better? No. Just like any drug, all it does is to dilute the truth about your own reality and who and what you truly are. Can you face that fact? Can you accept that fact? If you can, now what?

You know, there is a war going on in the Ukraine. Russia is decimating the people and the infrastructure of that country just because they didn't get their own way. The people in places like China and Iran and Afghanistan, and a lot of other locations, are having their lives and their potential torn apart due to authoritarian rule. Here in the U.S., our borders are being assaulted right now, on a scale never seen before, by those people who want to live the American dream. Do I understand their reason why? Of course, I do. They want what we have. But, what will be the cost to the U.S. from all of these people rushing into this country? Sure, maybe those people will have a better life, but what about the rest of us; the citizens and the taxpayers, what will it do to us?

If you want to think about some struggle that is taking place, think about those situations.

For any of us who have been in a family, (as most of us have), for any of us who have been in a relationship, you know there have been disagreements and fights. That's just the nature of the beast. Sometimes you just get pissed off at the person. Sometimes you dwell on what they are doing, how they are behaving, or what they have done to you. Other times you explode and yell. Maybe you even throw and brake things. That's just life. For most, they never take the fight to the street, however. They never broadcast it to the world. Sure, maybe other family members or friends or business associates or neighbors may hear the brawl, but it is lived and then it is gone. You lived it. Whomever you lived through it with, experienced it. Maybe someone else heard about it, but then it was over. That is life! That is your life! That is what you lived and lived through! That is and should be your life focus! To take the drug of diving into the life of someone else is a fool's passion because what does it equal? What does it mean to your life? Did it/does it make you a better person? No. At most, it simply makes you another person who proves you have nothing better to do than to think about someone else. It only illustrates that you are not realizing and focusing on your own flaws, your own limitation, and you trying to fix them and become a better person.

My thoughts... Next time you find yourself thinking about someone else—someone who actually means nothing to your life and to your own evolution, stop it. Focus on you. Focus on making your life, the life of those you know, and the world a better place. Stopped being dragged into taking the life-drug of thinking about people that have nothing to do with your existence. Choose to focus on the things that actually matter to your life. Redirect your thoughts to you focusing on you doing what you can do to make you and the overall world a better place.

*   *   *

15/Dec/2022 06:45 AM

When someone expresses that you have done something to hurt or damage their life what do you do? Do you strive to repair the damage or do you hide in your world of denial, excuses, and justifications?

Are You a Musician?
15/Dec/2022 06:38 AM

I don't know if you're a musician or not??? If you are, then you understand that, as a musician, you are always trying to find and/or create that perfect sound/that perfect note. You may play the same passage over and over and over again, just trying to get to the essence of that musical passage to find it/to play it perfectly.

This is very much like the understanding of Mantra meditation. If you know about this meditation technique you understand that the practitioner attempts to perfectly emulate the sound of that meditative word or words into order to evoke its cosmic meaning. From this, the zealot hopes to come to a level of true meditation leading to the ultimate goal of enlightenment.

I know some musicians try to write that perfect song. I know in my younger years, when I was spending a lot of time composing lyrics, I did that. In fact, I published a whole book with tons of my songs in it, The Lyrics.

But, as a musician, the search for that perfect note went way beyond that. I know I would play the guitar for hours upon hours when I was young; experimenting while trying to find the perfect combinations of notes. I worked with all kinds of different tunings, experimenting with the hope of finding that something new.

Yes, yes, I know, and I've said it as well, the notes have all already been played. But, as a musician, you really try to find your perfect expression of those notes.

I got into synthesizers very early on in my life. There was always something so untried and investigative with a synthesizer—something that you can find that maybe is sincerely New.

It's just like in the martial arts, the practitioner practices the same technique over and over and over again with the hopes of tracing that technique to its essence; the place where the martial artists may truly understand and master that one specific technique.

Most people in life do not strive to reach that level of inner-exploration in whatever it is that they do, however. They just do to get it done. Sure, some musicians are like that, as well. But, if you really/truly desire to get to the essence of that something—fully come to understand its everything, it really takes the time and the focus and the obsession to trace that whatever to its source and find that perfect note.

So, what is it you really care about? What is that one thing (or more) that genuinely causes you to reach a meditative mindset every time you partake? Think about it. Focus on it. Truly decide to follow it to its source and find that true inner perfection that can only be had in the deep permeation of that knowledge.

Find what you love. Follow it to its source. And, come to master that one specific thing, even if it is just one note played on a musical instrument. Try it. From this, you may experience an entirely new level of self-realization.

Almost-Almost Famous
and From Your Lips to God's Ears
14/Dec/2022 01:08 PM

There's the old staying, *"From your lips to God's ears."* I don't know the origin of that saying but its meaning is fairly clear. I think if more people thought about what they were saying and that if they considered that God was listening to what they were communicating maybe so much negativity would not be unleashed via people's mouths.

With that as a first-thought, let me continue…

I was heading over to a local Korean-owned market today to pick up some stuff for dinner. As I was walking through the store I realized, (as this is a fairly traditional Korean orientated market), that if you did not understand Korean cuisine, you may be a little freaked out as to what this market offered. They have stuff like a bunch of just dead fish piled up with their heads still on, live crabs roaming in a vat, several layers deep, and stuff like that. But, that's not the point. That's just one of the visuals of my day for you.

On my way over there, I had a few moments, so I stopped at the near-by thrift store. That's just my thing to do, when I have a moment, as you never know what you will find. Mostly, you/I find nothing, but you never know…

While I was doing my quick pass through the aisles, I noticed this one woman of obvious East Indian origin; at least ethnically. She was walking down each aisle so slowly and studying every element of every item. The thing that brought my attention to her was that she was one of those people who were/are very exaggerated in their gum chewing. You know those people who just chew their gum so expressively.

As I found myself looking at her, just then, I got a text from a friend of mine quoting someone saying something about me somewhere online. God, I hate that stuff and those reminders! I wish people would stop sending me that kind of stuff. Yeah, I get it, (knowing me), they think it's funny. But, I'm all about the positive, not the negative. I just don't need to hear that stuff. Anyway, he finished up his text, *"You're so famous."* Of course, he was being facetious, but it set me to thinking...

I jokingly replied, like I always do, *"I'm Almost-Almost Famous."*

Of course, when I say that, I'm referencing to that great movie, *"Almost Famous."* It's been in rotation on one of the many movie services I subscribe to, so I've been watching a little bit of it here or there of late; when I'm flipping channels. Good movie!

I actually auditioned for a Cameron Crowe film, the writer/director of that movie, way back in the day when I was doing a lot of auditioning and stuff. It was kind of funny. My agent called me up and told me of the time and place. I get there, Crowe said, *"Hi,"* to me as I passed him leaving the building as I was coming in, though he wasn't the one actually doing the auditioning. I signed in and got called into the office after a few minutes. The casting director looked at my picture and then looked at me, *"Where's this guy?"*

To tell the backstory, I didn't know what headshot my agent had sent. ...As I never did. This was back in the day, long before the digital age, where agents actually had their runners take their actor's headshots over to casting directors when they thought they fit the role.

Anyway, though I never really thought about it until that moment, the photo he sent made me look overweight. I always have worn clothes that are a bit too big. I continually buy my pants and my shirts and my sport coats a size or two larger than are needed. It's just more comfortable that way. But, in looking at that photograph, with new eyes, I saw that my shirt, and the way it draped over me, made me look fat. Plus, I had a full beard in that shot and I arrived at the audition clean-shaven. They were looking for a big burly guy, that I was not. At least not at that moment.

Didn't get the role... Oh well, I did get to say, *"Hi,"* to Cameron Crowe.

The thinking about that sent me to pondering a posting I saw from one of my friends this morning. I'm not going to say his name, but the guy is truly, *"Famous."* He created an important franchise.

Anyway, way back in the day, (again), we were at this big martial art event. I used to be invited to those type of things all the time. It's back when I was writing a lot of magazine articles and my martial art orientated books were being published and finding a large audience. That was before I became more-and-more of a recluse and stopped going to those and other events. I just found that it became very hard to trust anybody and I just got tired of being fucked over. Anyway...

We, he and I, were walking around this event and everybody wanted to take a picture with me. *"Master Shaw, can I take a picture with you?"* *"Sure, but call me, Scott."* I kept telling everyone who this guy was and that they really needed to take a photograph with him, as he had really done something BIG. But, that was back in the early days of digital photography and you could only take a very few photos with your camera before your disk was full. So, most declined.

My time at that level of notoriety eventually came to an end. I believed, back then, that I would continue to climb the ladder. But, as is the case with most, that did not happen. I'm sure of the few people that did take a photo with my friend, they are glad that they did, and the ones who didn't, probably wish that they had as his career had a big resurgence a few years later.

Anyway, so he we are, trapped in the world we are trapped in. There are people, like the young woman discussed at the beginning of this piece, locked in the world of nothing better to do. ...Slowly wandering the aisles of a thrift store, trying to find some meaning in items that hold none. There are those people who say things about people like me online, for who knows what reason??? Don't they have anything better to think about? There are people like my friend, who still to this day rocks the world with his creation. Then, there's people like me, the Almost-Almost Famous who just try to run away from it all and create art in a world that is not dominated solely by the misplaced, untruthful, judgmental, and hurtful words of people who must have something better to talk about, yet they choose to mumble my name from their lips.

"From your lips to God's ears." Think about it.

* * *
14/Dec/2022 07:48 AM

What do you do when someone says something about you that's not true and other people believe them?

* * *
14/Dec/2022 07:34 AM

At what point are you strong enough to undo what you have done?

Treat Everyone with Respect
13/Dec/2022 12:46 PM

I was having lunch with a friend of mine the other day. The server brought us our food and I said, *"Thank you, sir."* After he left the table my friend, who's a Hollywood Up-and-Comer, said to me, *"You really shouldn't call people sir. What you're doing by saying that is implying that they are more than you."* My response, *"They are."*

Everybody deserves respect! I call people, *"Sir,"* all the time, everywhere I go. I want them to know that they are respected. I want them to know that they are doing an important job. I want them to understand that they are living an honorable life.

…Perhaps the saddest thing in all of this is that this is not the first time I've heard a statement such as this.

Whenever anyone refers to me as, *"Sir,"* I always respond, *"Just call me Scott."* But, that's me saying the words. You do not have to refer to me in any superior fashion just because of your job or your whatever. That's me saying it. To them, however, they deserve the respect.

…I even have my martial arts students just call me, Scott. Just because I've been involved with the martial arts longer than most of them have been alive, that does not mean I am anything more than they are.

That's one of the things I really dislike about the world wide web. There is so much disrespect going on. I am constantly reminded of it, and it makes me just want to Sign-Off all the time. Whether fortunately or unfortunately, however, it is one of my main ways of communicating with people. So???

All this being said, we all really need to respect everyone. If you are being disrespectful to anyone, in any way, stop it! What makes you any more than them? What make you any better than them? What gives you the right to critique and/or judge their life, their lifestyle, or their means of employment?

For all the people who read this blog, I am sure I am not saying anything that you don't already know. I am fairly sure it is not you doing anything disrespectful. But, there are those people out there who do—those who are condescending and disrespectful of the life and the lifestyle of other people. Those are the one who need to rethink their drink. And, believe me, I let my friend know what I thought about his ideology.

In closing, stop saying judgmental, hurtful, and disrespectful things. Stop believing that you are something more than any other person. Maybe that person you are commenting about has not been provided with the opportunities that you have. Maybe they have not been afforded the life choices you have enjoyed. Maybe they have lived a different life path or lifestyle than you have experienced. No matter what the case or the cause, everyone deserves respect. Let this fact begin with you.

You're Old
13/Dec/2022 07:39 AM

    I was walking to my car yesterday afternoon. I noticed that this young neighborhood boy was riding his pedal-less push bike up and down the streets. His parents, an interracial couple, were standing nearby telling him to be careful. Just as I got to my car, he pulls up behind me. *"Excuse me, you're old."* Those were the exact words that instantly came out of his mouth. This statement, of course, made me smile. I immediately responded, *"Is that a good thing?"* I could tell my question threw the boy as he was obviously trying to throw a shot my direction. Where someone so young would have come up with the idea to come at people he didn't know like that, I have no idea. But, he did. In any case, I could see he was searching his mind for an answer and he said, *"Well… I'm five years old and I'm young."* At that point, his parents called to him and he moved along. Interesting…

    I later told my lady of the experience. We both laughed and we both agreed that if we had said something like that to an adult, when we were young, and our parents heard as the young boy's parents had, we would have been disciplined. I am sure my father would have, (at least), given me a hard smack in the face. My lady said, he probably would have broken your bike—that would be the end of that and then you would have understood what was right and wrong. She may be right. *"You're old,"* went back and forth between us for a few hours last night.

    Age is an interesting thing. Personally, when I was young, I never expected to live this long. I thought I would probably end up knifed in some backstreet of Bangkok or something like that. So, for me, telling me I'm old is a compliment. Every day I spend alive is a gift.

    I watched the Robert Downey Jr. documentary he made about his father, Robert Downey Sr. last night, (though he wasn't the director). It's called. *"Sr."* Good piece. I suggest you watch it if you have the opportunity. Its' on Netflix. Not only is it an interesting exploration into age and aging and eventually dying, but it's a great view into the filmmaking career of the man and his involvement in the *Absurdist's Movement* of filmmaking.

In the doc., they show some clips from some of his films. Back in the day, I watched some of his movies. I never found that kind of in-your-face humor very interesting, however. But, that's just me. He obviously did have an audience. The one thing I did come away with was, at least in regard to filmmaking and filmmakers is that, people have often questioned me, if I thought if I had brought *Zen Filmmaking* up in another era, say the 1960s, when the understanding of freeform art was more prevalent, would I have found greater acceptance? I always kind of dismiss questions like that as I am one of those people who tries to live in the NOW. But, seeing those film clips in that doc., it did make me realize that, yes, if I did what I do back then, it may have been more accepted. But, I was just a kid. A kid, like that young boy yesterday.

Which brings me back to the subject of age. It seems people always run from their age. They hide behind hair dyes, plastic surgery, Botox, and just lying about their age. But, all of that never changes the reality of the reality.

Think about when you were young, every adult was old. Though many/most do not want to hear this fact, that is the reality of projection—particularly the projection of a child. So, when do you become old? I don't know? Physically, yes, I may be old. But, I feel so young. I think it's a choice. You can be old if you want to. Or, you can be young until you are not. Sure, that may not change someone else's definition of you. But, their definition does not need to make you what they expect you to be.

Are you what someone else defines you as? Or, are you the definition of yourself? Think about it.

Yoga: Merging with God
12/Dec/2022 10:04 AM

  I am often perplexed by the people who claim yoga is an integral part of their life, but they do not even comprehend the true essence of yoga. They love the postures. Why? Because they are doing something. They love the way it makes them feel. Why? Because it causes energy to move through their body; similar to the way other physical exercises may make them feel. But, you speak to them about the actual definition of yoga, *"Merging with God,"* and their faces go blank or they proclaim that is not why I am there. Explain that the entire concept, definition, practice, and ultimate goal of yoga is based in the Hindu understanding of life and they proclaim, *"I'm a Christian."*

  I remember I was teaching the physical aspects of yoga, known as Hatha Yoga and Pranayama, at this Buddhist Center in L.A. back in the late 1970s. A new manager of the facility came on-board and he was speaking to all of the people, who, like I, had been previously asked to teach classes at the location. He stated, *"I don't want any of this Satchidananda or Sivananda nonsense going on here."* Wow, that statement threw me. Swami Satchidananda was my teacher and Swami Sivananda was his. Both, were two of the most influential figures in the dissemination of yoga at the time. Yet, here was this man, who obviously knew very little about the true essence of yoga, throwing out this blanket statement. I guess he was just some sort of established management type which is why the Buddhist monk who oversaw the facility had brought him on-board. Was he walking the spiritual path? I don't know? Didn't sound like it, however.

  The point being is that, if at the top level of a business that is spreading the knowledge of spirituality outwards to the world is managed by someone who doesn't understand the root essence of one of their most popular classes, how can the average student, seeking to gain new knowledge, be properly schooled on the subject and the techniques? Me, after that group meeting, I never went back, though I did receive several calls asking me to resuming teaching my classes, from that man, as they were very popular. I was nice in my declining, as I always try to be. But, what I wanted to say was, *"I thought you didn't want any of this Satchidananda or Sivananda nonsense going on."*

I don't know what is going on or what is being taught in the hatha yoga classes of today. I haven't attended any or really watched any of them being taught. Through the grape vine and via extended family members I have, however, listened to some discussion of the techniques that are being communicated. What I never hear is anything about the true essence of all forms of yoga—what they are actually meant to supply the practitioner with. Namely, a pathway of mental and physical purification and betterment leading to a deeper realization of God.

When I became involved with the various aspects of yoga in the 1960s, and through the 1970s, the focus on it was very clear. The true understanding of it was being broadcast. Somewhere in the 1980s, the mindset of the populist began to change and interest in yoga feel away. Then, in the 1990s, yoga again reemerged and began to move to the forefront of the talked-about and the practiced. As it remerged, however, its focus had completely changed. It became all about what the postures can do for you physically. And sure, maybe a minute or two of meditation practice was thrown in at the end of the class, but its essence, its true meaning, had been lost.

I'm speaking about yoga here as an example. And, it is a good one. But, think about the overall essence and truth of the truth of life. How much of what you are presented with, how much of what you are taught, how much of what you practice is based in the elemental knowledge possessed by the founders of that whatever? And, how much of it has been watered-down to the degree where all it has become is a business and a way for people to make money and maybe a method for its teachers to gain that some sort of ego-filled something that they could not find naturally present within themselves.

Ask yourself, who is teaching what and why? Ask yourself, what are you learning and why? Is what you are being taught the truth and the true intended essence of that whatever? Or, is what you are learning nothing more than someone's diluted something that is missing what the true spirit and principal of that subject is all about?

Scott-ish
09/Dec/2022 09:50 AM

I made a joke the other day, while speaking to a friend, *"I'm trying not to be so Scott-ish."* What I was saying was that I was trying to move away from the way I commonly behave.

For the record, my heritage is Scottish, so I had to emphasize, *"Scott-ish,"* so they would understand what I actually meant.

Think about it, think about how you behave. We all behave in a manner that is uniquely unique to ourselves. For some, they emulate a very good, positive being. For others, not so much. Sure, we can all claim that this or that happened to us causing is to become what we have become, but what does that all mean? It just means that we are not taking responsibly for ourselves in this moment or over an entire lifetime.

We do what we do based on upon what we do. We behave the way we behave based upon what we choose to do. But, without a conscious effort, nothing ever changes.

Think about yourself. Visualize how you behave. How do you behave? Few people ever take the time to study this. They just do. Some even proclaim, *"That's just me."* But, who made you, you? Who taught you how to behave in that manner? Moreover, who is in control of the way you behave? If it isn't you, if it isn't you making a choice, then who is it?

If you look at the life of most people; though they get older through time, few ever change their life patterns and/or their behavior. Few people ever actually evolve. Why is this? Because they do not have the mind to try. They simply allow themselves to BE, guided by whatever it is they are feeling, motivate by that deep unexplored unknown that is the, *"I,"* within themselves.

How about you? How much do you know about why you are the way you are? How much honest study do you put into this topic? If you are like most, the answer to that question is very little.

Most people set goals for themselves to achieve. They are physical things like graduating from school, getting a specific job, making money, buying a car or a house, getting married and having a family, and all the stuff like that. But, those are all things. None of those, *"Things,"* are based in the study of Self and who you Truly Are.

Who are you? Why are you? Why do you do what you do? Why do you hold the personality that you possess? Why do you behave in the manner you project?

If you do not know the answer to these questions, if you cannot take control over those aspects of your life, then who holds control over your life: you or that vast unknown something Out There which you have not taken the time to find out what it actually is?

You can do whatever it is you want to do in life, you can behave in any manner you see fit, but if you do not choose to study and then take control over those elements of your life, then how self-aware are you?

* * *

07/Dec/2022 01:55 PM

Is your today defined by your yesterday or is your today defining your tomorrow?

We're All Gonna Die Someday Lord
07/Dec/2022 08:03 AM

"We're all gonna die someday lord." If I may, let me quote the Kasey Chambers song…

I think back to the later days of my friend, Donald G. Jackson's life. He really enjoyed going out and seeing live music. Particularly that of the alt country genre. We would spend many an evening in dingy clubs around L.A., listening to bands that no one ever heard of. Some of them were really good.

There was this one night where we went to see the great Australian songstress, Kasey Chambers at the Roxy. We got there a bit early, and I introduced Don to her. I had previously exposed him to her music, and he was a big fan.

She was going to do her soundcheck and Don was hungry, as he tended to be, so we headed over to Barney's Beanery to grab a bite to eat. By the time we got back, Kasey was already on stage. Don walked up to a guy, not realizing it was Dwight Yoakam, and asked what time she went on. I smiled as this happened, as Don was also a big fan of Dwight and the Bakersfield's style of Country that he played. *"That was Dwight Yoakam,"* Don exclaimed, after he got his answer. He tended to be a bit of a fan boy. *"Yeah,"* I said…

Don apologized for making me miss a bit of the show. …Didn't bother me. I'm more about friendships than live music. At least I was by that point in my life.

Back then, at least on the airwaves, alternative music was a bit hard to find. For those of us who were part of the first-generation of MTV music, it used to be this understood secret that if you stayed up late at night, they would play the more obscure music videos. It felt like some sort of achievement when you saw that one you had never seen before, created by some obscure artist. Now, of course, everything is on-line, and you can just call it up if you know what you're looking for. But, not back then.

Near the end of the show, Kasey played her song, *"We're all gonna die someday lord."* I looked at Don, who was becoming more-and-more frail as he was dying from leukemia, and I said, *"That's easy to say when your twenty-four,"* which Kasey was at that point in her life. Don agreed. He lived for less than a year after that show.

You know, I believe you really need to hold your Life Moments close to your heart. You really need to do the best that you can with the time that you have. You really need to be nice and always be caring and help, never hurt. I know everyone says it, but it is all so short—life is so short of a time. Look around you, listen to the news, the famous and the news-worthy are dying all the time. That is just a reminder, because someone close to you may not be knocking on heaven's door right now; but they will be very soon, you will be.

Live your life as best as you can. Love you family and your friends and your pets and your car and your things and everybody and everything. When you're alive, you've got to feel! You've got to make those memories because when that friend or family member of yours has passed, you will be the only left who remembers. When you're gone, those you knew, interacted with, and loved will be the only ones that will remember you and those moments that you shared together. What will they remember?

* * *
07/Dec/2022 08:03 AM

Do something nice today.

* * *

06/Dec/2022 04:46 PM

If making you more means you have to make someone less, you have missed the entire point of success.

* * *
06/Dec/2022 03:49 PM

Who knocked on your door when you weren't home and you never knew who came a-knock'n?

* * *
06/Dec/2022 08:17 AM

Just because you don't get it does not mean that it can't be understood.

Finding Your Meditative Mind
06/Dec/2022 07:43 AM

For millennia, the science of meditation has been known to be one of the best practices that can be employed by the individual to not only calm their body and their mind but to cause them to encounter new understandings about Self and the Cosmos. Though this has long been known, how many people throughout the centuries have actually practiced meditation? How many people have sat down, focused, and caused their mind to become silent? Very few. How about you, have you/do you practice meditation?

The one thing that can be said about someone who practices meditation is that they care more about developing a deeper understanding of themselves and reality than does the person who shuns this process. This fact is not bad or good, it is simply a fact. And, this is what sets an individual who meditates apart from those who do not.

Most people who do not meditate have their reasons why. I'm not here to question those reasons, I am just here to ask them to question their reasons. For questioning one's life reality is perhaps the first step in coming to a greater understanding of Self and True Reality.

As has been handed down throughout the centuries, the basic understanding of meditation is based upon two concepts: Dharana and Dhyana. Here's a bit from one of my books:

Dharana means, *"Concentration."* This is the first step of meditation—for without the ability to acutely focus your thinking mind you will not possess the capability to truly meditate.

The practice of Dharana teaches you to guide your mind into a one-pointedness not known to the average individual. Dharana teaches you to not let passing thoughts control you—leading to desires, emotions, and anxieties about situations which are not existent in the present moment. Dharana refines your mind to the degree that when you sit to meditate, you sit to meditate and will not be frustrated by a lack of focus.

Dhyana means, *"Meditation."* Meditation has long been understood to be the primary component to refining a human being and linking them with divine consciousness.

Meditation is much more than simple concentration. Meditation witnesses you, very consciously, placing your one-pointed focus upon an image, object, or an energy that represents the supreme being or ultimate reality. To achieve this, as a Christian you may focus upon a mental image of Jesus. As a Hindu, you may visualize an incarnation of Vishnu, or perhaps the god Shiva, Kali, Hanuman, or Ganesha. If you are a Buddhist, the focus of your meditation may be upon the essence of Siddhartha Guatama, the Sakyamuni Buddha. If you are an individual who believes that God is an undefined source of pure energy and knowledge, your attention may be placed upon a mental image of pure white light or very consciously watching your breath, as it enters and exits your body—as this is what links your human body to this physical life. Therefore, this presents you with the opportunity to advance your spiritual being to the higher planes of consciousness. In whatever format, what sets meditation apart from concentration is focus.

All that being said, meditation does not have to be a Thing that you must work at to achieve; as that is perhaps the biggest reason that some people are tuned-off to meditation. In can be simply allowing your mind to BE.

For example, have you ever been doing something and you realize a lot of time has passed and you did not even notice due to the fact you were so focused on what you were doing? I believe we've all had that happen to us. But, is that meditation? Perhaps? But, more than likely that is simply Dharana, concentration.

Meditation arises from a different mindset. It arises in a state of peace where the mind is allowed to be calm.

Think of a time when you were at the beach, looking at the waves, in the mountains, watching the wind blow through the trees, in the desert, studying the vastness of the horizon. In these, and other cases, your mind is allowed to find its own silence, its own meditation.

This is the thing about meditation, it does not have be accomplished by formally sitting with your legs crossed. It can occur anywhere, anytime. But, you must choose to encounter it.

For me, in some of my Zen Films, I present a target of meditation. Maybe it is a fountain of running water or the waves impacting the shore of the beach. If you can just be silent in those moments, meditation can be found anywhere.

If you want to sit in Zazen, you can do that. You can watch your breath, you can chant a mantra, you can just close your eyes and turn off your mind. If you want to allow nature (or even the chaos of the city) to cause you to guide your mind into a state of contemplative focus, you can do that, as well. But, if you do not meditate you will never understand the profound silence that may be experienced and known within your own mind. If you do not know it via practice, you cannot instantly step into when you need to center and/or calm your mind. Without meditation you are cursed to be under the control of all thing's life—some of which are not that enjoyable. Without meditation you can never know the profound wisdom experienced by beings like the Buddha.

However you do it, however you find your silence, if you don't do it, you have not done it. Thus, you will forever by defined by the ways of the world and you will never know the truth that can be witness in meditative stillness. Choose to meditate. If you do it for a moment, five minutes, a hour, or more, believe me, it will change your understanding of your reality.

Zen Filmmaking: It's a Spiritual Process
05/Dec/2022 09:45 AM

I recently wrote a piece about one of those attack ads that a couple of content creators on YouTube did on a (kinda) Zen Film. Thankfully, after I contacted them, they pulled *Zen Filmmaking* out of their title, as they themselves had claimed it was used solely to get more followers. But, all this and all that brings us to the part and parcel of *Zen Filmmaking* and the essential essence of the craft that everybody either doesn't understand or seems to forget. *Zen Filmmaking* is a spiritual process. It is not just some form of guerrilla filmmaking. Yes, *Zen Filmmaking* may, during some productions, exist in and on the level of microbudget filmmaking, but that is not its essence nor is it its core. It is all about the process of the creation of a film based in the purest sense of mysticism.

The entire reason Zen is referenced in the title of this style of filmmaking is that it evokes the essence of Zen. It is designed to emulate the space of Mushin, No Mind, the free-flowing nature of allowing all things to be as they are, following the path of least resistance, and the hope for anything to not be anything but what it is.

It's easy to criticize. Anybody can look at Anything and easily find fault if that is what they are watching for. But, people who operate on that level of life are existing in a space defined by unenlightened negativity. Sure, many people live their entire existence operating from this life-perspective. But, what does that give back to humanity? Does it make anything any better? No. All it does is to unleash hate. But, what is hate? It is one person casting their harsh judgment onto something else. Whether this is unleashed in a small or a large dose, the outcome is still the same: pain and suffering. The embracing of hurtful negativity, how does that make any level of life any better? It does not.

Whenever I see or hear *Zen Filmmaking* being discussed by people of this mindset, I always witness the same levels of criticism. But what these people never understand is the dome of magic that takes place for those of us on the set. The freedom of artistic spontaneity. The amazement at perfect situations presenting themselves to us. The cinematic art that is created simply by allowing ourselves to be free in our creative portrayals.

I'm not going to go into detail, spelling out the tenets of *Zen Filmmaking,* in this little ditty, for I have done that for decades in other places. It's all out there if you feel like reading it. What I will reemphasis AGAIN is, *Zen Filmmaking* is a spiritual process. With Zen at its core, and art at its heart, it is a way of displaying an individual's cinematic vision in the most spiritually-based, art-filled manner possible.

Sure, as a human being you may love or hate what has been produced. That's human nature. Nobody likes all the art that they encounter. But, if the actual point of a Zen Film's inception is missed or misrepresented, or simply placed in the realm of something to be judged, the spiritual essence of that Zen Film is lost. It is lost to the judgmental mind of one or more people and from this the cinematic enlightenment that could be found in that production is simply cast to the realms of the lower mind where Satori or Nirvana may never be embraced.

It's like what Donald G. Jackson used to say in interviews and stuff, *"I don't think most people could do what Scott and I do. They need structure. We just get out there and create."* And, isn't that what true art is based upon; instantaneous inspiration and creation? I mean, many people base their criticism of *Zen Filmmaking* on the fact that it does not use screenplays. But, think how many bad independent films you have seen that were based on a script.

So, next time you're watching a Zen Film, (if you ever do), understand its foundation. In fact, next time you watch any film or look at any art, seek to step beyond your own lower mind of judgement, witness the piece for what it truly is, and experience the spirituality that goes into creating any piece of art.

Your mind, your judgement, should never be the definition of any piece of art. For that denies all that it truly is. It negates the artist's vision.

Spiritually is everywhere if you simply open your eyes. I am sure in your deepest mind you too speak to God in your own way. Is the way of God based upon you judging all things that you see, all things that you like or don't like? No. God is the pure light of the all-encompassing everything. A truly spiritual person never judges. Let that be your guide.

Remember, *Zen Filmmaking,* is a spiritual process. That is its essence. Never allow a Zen Film to be denigrated by the words of those who refused to understand its elemental foundations.

* * *
04/Dec/2022 07:24 AM

If you can allow something negative that is done to you to cause you to do something positive, the world becomes an immensely better place.

Take a Photograph of Nothing
04/Dec/2022 07:19 AM

"Does the world really look better through rose-colored glasses?"

I was walking down the street with a friend of mine and this is a joking question they asked me, referencing that age old saying, as I was wearing this pair of rose-tinted glasses that I own. I took my glasses off and handed them over to them and said, *"Take a look. Tell me what you think."*

They didn't actually put them on because they are prescription. What they did do, however, was to take out their phone and hold the glasses in front of the lens of the camera on their phone and they snapped a shot. *"Let me see!"* She showed it to me. It was great! I mean, there we were, on a street I had been on a million times, just a street like any street anywhere; nothing special about it at all. But, through my rose-colored glasses the photograph became, (I don't know), so much of something. Really beautiful.

I know that there are colored lens filters. I used to use them when I was doing creative photograph, with film, back in the '70s and the '80s. And sure, there are all those aftereffects you can use nowadays. But somehow, by just holding my glasses up, that photograph became all so Zen. A perfect photograph.

My realization was, you really need to take photographs of nothing—nothing special anyway. Just those average scenes from average life. If you have some color-tinted glasses, sure put them in front of the lens. If you don't, snap that shot anyway. Take it home and give it a tweaking. You never known; you may have taken the perfect photograph. But, if you don't take it, it will have never been taken.

In answer to the question, Yes, the world really does look better through rose-colored glasses. I saw the proof.

Hurt Equals Hurt
03/Dec/2022 08:01 AM

First if all, let me begin by saying, I believe that anyone who consciously unleashes hurt on any level really needs to take a long hard look at themselves. Secondarily, I believe that anyone who is the benefactor of someone who unleashes hurt on any level really needs to take a long hard look at themselves.

Hurt equals hurt. Initial hurt only hurts the person who is being hurt and then, from that hurt, causes them to possibly react which causes more hurt. Answer? Don't hurt!

Think about a time when you said something bad about a person, did something bad to a person, or enacted any of those negative hurtful behaviors. Why did you do it? Why did you behave in that manner? Did it truly make your life any better; you hurting them?

People always question, *"Why me,"* when something negative happens to them. How often do they look to what they have done, in the past, and whom they have done it to, when they are hit with a karmic blow? Rarely. Why is this? Because most people live in a self-centered realm of their own reality where the only person they can truly feel for is themselves.

Think about a time when someone did something that hurt you. How did that feel? How did that cause you to react? In many cases, it causes a person to go on a counterattack. But, what does that equal? Additional counterattacks. Thus, the hurt never stops.

Certainly, there has been decades upon decades of studies going into why certain individuals exhibit abusive behavior. It is no secret that one of the common conclusions is that this is due to that person having encountered abusive behavior at the hands of their family, peers, or the society that surrounds them. Thus, deep in their being, they have come to unconsciously believe that is the way to act. Of course, from an analytical perspective we all know that this is not the case, but on that internal intrinsic level most people are not aware enough to study the source of their violence. They just unleash it.

For people who grew up in my generation, and those before, corporal punishment was the norm. You did something wrong and you got hit. Even as late at when I was in middle school, if you did something wrong, the assistant principal would take you into his office, take out a paddle, and smack you hard on the butt. I got a few of those. Of course, I got back at him by flattening his tires and keying his car. But, there again, hurt equals hurt.

Look at the case of Brian Wilson of *Beach Boys* fame. He is considered one of the greatest and most revolutionary composers and producers of the 1960s. His father smacked him in the head so hard that it fractured his ear drum, causing him to lose hearing in one ear. Not right, but that was the norm. What did he do so wrong that he deserved to lose hearing in one ear?

Today, though many parents no longer follow the pathway of hurting their children via physical violence, things like psychological hurt and hurt via other subtle methods is still very-very prevalent.

There are many levels of hurt that go beyond the physical. There is the hurt of theft. There is the hurt of being judgmental. There is the hurt of toying with an individual's emotions. There is the hurt of undermining a person. There is the hurt of being untruthful about a person. There is the hurt of using a person. There is the hurt of throwing an individual under the bus. And, the list goes on. Again, what does hurting anyone on any level equal? Nothing but more hurt. And, if an individual feels empowered by their ability to hurt someone else, there is nothing that can be said about them but they are a bad person and should be shunned.

Some people judge and say very negative, untruthful things about people. Why do they do that? What causes them to believe that they should possess this power? Is it a god given right? No. Is it due to the First Amendment of the Constitution here in the U.S.? No. It is all based in their need to hurt. They are the one instigating the hurt. They are the one who has decided to try to hurt. Who else is to blame?

On the deeper level, why do certain people behave in this fashion? Most likely, it is because they are operating from a position of hurt. They have been hurt. They have come to believe, (as unconscious as that belief may be), that they have the right to hurt. But, what good ever comes from any of that? None.

In closing, you can be the impetuous for change. You can be the sourcepoint of unleashing no more hurt. You can stop hurt in its tracks by not supporting it and/or those who unleash hurt. And, if you find yourself thinking about hurting anyone or anything, catch yourself. Become that bigger, better, and more conscious individual. Stop the pattern of hurt!

Intension Verses Expectation
02/Dec/2022 03:24 PM

What is your intension? No really, what is your intention? Why are you about to do what you are about to do? Why did you do what you just did?

These are things that very few people ever think about except on the most superficial level. *"I do it because it makes me feel good." "I do it to make money." I do it because I want someone to like me" "I do it to hurt someone."* But, those are all just things. They are not the deep-rooted cause of your intension.

Do you ever truly study the motivation for your intention? Most people do not.

Is there a problem in this? Well, yes. The problem is, all of this stuff gets done without anyone ever really knowing why. People are helped, people are hurt, people are loved, people are hated, actions are taken, but no one ever really knows why.

Think about a time when someone did something to you that you did not like. Why did they do it? Sure, they may have some superficial answer, but is that the true answer? Most likely, it is not. What they did was more than likely motivated by some deep wound that they hold in the deepest realms of their being. A wound that they, themselves, may not even be clear about. It's there. They may try to expound that hurt onto others due to it. It may cause them to take actions. But, without deep self-study they have no real realization about the fact that it causes them to do what they do and behave in the manner that they behave.

If you look at life, if you study people's behavior, there are stereotypes. In many cases, stereotypes are true because a person exhibiting a certain characteristic behaves like others who possess similar foundational programing. This is all very rudimentary. With this as a basis, who is saying what about whom and who is doing what to whomever? Look deeply at who is doing the doing, listening to who is saying the saying, and you can develop deep insight into their motivations. Insight, that they themselves, might not even possess, because an individual looking at, and admitted to who they truly are, is a very difficult process.

Do you ever think about any of this? Or, do you simply follow the pattern of behavior that you have evolved into explicating?

You see, people who do not known the reason for their intensions look only to their expectation for guidance. They focus on what they want and that is that. They expect what they expect and if they do not get it then they blame, criticize, and attack as a method to denunciate others for their own unfulfilled expectations.

That's the easy way out. It is so much easier to look outside then to gaze inside.

But, why do they want what they want? Why do you want what you want? And, what does it cause you do to? Moreover, what does it say about you?

What you want is defined by the drug you are looking to take to make you feel better about yourself.

How do you act towards others? What do you say about other people? What does what you think and feel about others, cause you to do? Do you ever think about any of this at all? If you don't, that may make you one of the many, but it will also cause you to do and say hurtful things, motivated only by what you refuse to look at, locked deeply within yourself.

So, the next time you see someone casting their expectations onto someone else, the next time you hear hurtful or judgmental words of criticism being cast onto someone, take a deep look at who is doing the saying and the doing. Who are they? Can you see who they truly are? Can you understand why they are doing what they are doing, even if they cannot?

More importantly, study yourself. Anytime you think a negative thought, possibly leading you to negative words or actions, catch yourself. Be more than your lower self. Find out who you are, why you think as you think, leading to why you do what you do. If nothing else, by being honest with yourself and truly knowing yourself you will be able to see what has caused you to do what you have done and maybe, just maybe, in that knowing you can fix all that is broken, all that you have broken, and all that is broken within yourself.

* * *
02/Dec/2022 09:36 AM

Everybody wants you to do something for them but what are they willing to do for you?

Kickboxer for Hire
01/Dec/2022 02:52 PM

Here's an interesting piece of Scott Shaw history for you that I came across this morning. It's a script I wrote called, *Kickboxer for Hire.*

To tell the story, a friend of mine, (who probably wants to remain nameless), contacted me and told me about this woman he had met that hoped to produce a martial arts movie. We met her, in association with the man she wanted to direct the film, and somebody else, I forget who that other person was??? She lived in a very nice house, talked the talk, and was apparently married to some studio exec., so it all seemed on the level.

We all spoke a bit and my friend and I were given the task to write the screenplay. It eventually came around to fact that my friend and I were also to star in the film. Sounded good to me!

My friend, who was a screenwriter, probably planned that we would do one of those back-and-forth Hollywood things and work our way through the script as a team. That's not how I work, however. I went home and wrote the script. I gave it to him the next day at this restaurant called, The Kettle, in Manhattan Beach, where we used to meet sometimes. He was obviously surprised. I thought he would take it home, tear it part, flip it around, do this or that to it, and add his changes. But, he really didn't do that. He just gave it back with a minor proofread.

Anyway, with a script, a leading cast, a producer, and a director, we were all set to go. The lady, the producer, finally got around to telling us that she had access to a large stock of 16mm film that she got somehow??? So, she wanted to shoot the film on 16mm. Fine with me! The director, who was a young film school grad, refused, however. He would only work in 35mm. So, with this and with that, the project fell apart. Welcome to Hollywood.

My friend was pissed. Me, whatever… I was used to this kind of Industry BS by this point in time. This was not the first time that I had been promised a deal, wrote a script, and then nothing came from it.

Of course, this is the abbreviated story of the story… But, you get the point.

This script, like so many others in Hollywood, has sat around forever. Is it one of my better screenplays? No, not really. It was one created to fill the ideas and mindset hopes of our producer, drawing upon the popularity of kickboxing at the time, and embracing that whole, *"Rocky,"* fighter overcoming adversity sort of thing.

Kickboxer for Hire. Here's the link to it if you feel like wasting some time and reading all or part of it. Due to the whole internet auto-formatting thing, it's not in perfect screenplay format. And, it was transferred from that ancient MAC word-processing program ClarisWorks. Just keep that in mind. Enjoy!!!

When the Strange Things Happen
01/Dec/2022 08:08 AM

I was putting dinner together last night. I was moving the cooking tray, with the food on it, into the oven. I've done that a million times. No problem. But, this time, last night, for some strange/unknown reason, the glass cutting board I was using somehow magically stunk to the bottom of the cooking tray. I didn't notice this, and as I was moving the tray to the oven, SMASH, the cutting board fell, hit the floor, and there was a million shards of glass everywhere.

Now, this is one of those things that no one wants to deal with. I mean, this was going to be a big mess to clean up.

Me, I popped the food into the oven, grabbed a broom, and started to sweep. Then, I get the vacuum cleaner. This all taking a lot of time. I mean, you don't want to get a little piece of glass in your foot or anything like that.

Of course, my cats are all interested in what's going on and stuff like that. But, I had to shoo them away as I didn't want them to step on the everywhere glass.

It took some time, but I got it cleaned up.

In the closing segment of all this annoyance and nonsense, I notice that a bunch of the glass had shattered in my cat's drinking bowl. Of course, I was going to clean that out. But, in looking at it, the shattered glass in the glass bowl, it made such a perfect expression of visual art. It is something that as an artist, I wish I could create. But, it was created for me. Of course, I took a photo of it before I cleaned out their drinking bowl.

Through all the nonsense and bother I was at least left with this photograph of naturally occurring art. Well, maybe better put, accidentally occurring art.

I believe you have to look for the art in everything. I mean, all kinds of nonsense happens to all of us all the time. Life will be going along all-good and then SMASH, the glass cutting board hits the floor. But, if you can find art in that moment, at least it will not have all been a waste. At least something may be created that will make the accident meaningful.

* * *
01/Dec/2022 07:43 AM

With your eyes focused on the world, all you can see is the world.

With your eyes closed in the silence of meditation, the essence of everything may be known.

* * *
30/Nov/2022 05:20 PM

If money doesn't matter to you then money doesn't matter.

No Mind Verses Some Mind
30/Nov/2022 07:58 AM

In Zen Buddhism, the state of *Mushin* or No Mind is the sought-after space of existence. From meditation, to art, to the martial arts, onto living wholly and consciously in everyday life, the seeker of absolute awareness focuses on traveling to the place where they may exist in *Mushin*.

Why is this the desired state of consciousness? Because it is only in this place one can free themselves from all wordily constrains and encounter a state of absolute freedom in thought, movement, and action.

For the artist, they concentrate on this mindset to gain a perfection in each brush stroke. For the martial arts, they focus on obtaining this state so that their movements become the perfect form of meditation as they are not guided by any external hopes or desires. For the meditator, this state is sought so that they remove all limitations of desire, leading to karma, and thus are free to exist in the space of Pure Mind where all is set to the natural experience of Zen.

For thousands of years there have been those who pursue *Mushin*. Throughout those thousands of years, however, those number have been minuscule in comparison to those who seek a wordily existence. Where do you find yourself in this pursuit? Do you seek a silent mind or do you seek all that the world has to offer?

Most, seek the world. Some, seek at least some level of deeper consciousness. Very few devote their life to finding No Mind. Why is this? Because the benefits are not obvious. What do you gain by encountered Mushin? If you cannot even understand the concept, how can you come up with an answer to that question?

This is why so few pursue Deep Mind. This is why the world lives in a state of ongoing chaos. This is why you are happy, sad, elated, depressed, fat, skinny, broke, in-debt, drunk, high, angry, hurtful, selfish, and self-centered. You seek what is Out There but not what is In Here. In Japanese, this state of mind is known as, *Ushin,* the opposite of *Mushin.*

There is the old saying, *"You can live in the world but not of the world."* We all must find a way to survive. But, that does not mean that we have to do it in such a manner where we create negative karma.

Everyone knows what selfish and hurtful actions are. Yet, think about it, how many people know those definitions but do those things anyway? How many people applaud those who live in that state of mind? How about you?

There is another side to all of this. You can live in the world but not of the world. This is where Mushin may be encountered. You can do what you need to do to survive but you can do it from a space of Pure Mind. You can operate in the realm of the rejection of being called into external life-play. You can consciously be conscious. How do you do that? You just do that. It is a simple as that.

People confuse things like meditation, the arts, the martial arts, and living a spiritual lifestyle as doing something. But then, it becomes a, *"Thing."* It becomes something that you must strive to do to perfection. But, think about it, if you allow all things to be perfect within themselves, doesn't everything find its own space of flawlessness? If you don't try, you don't have to try. You can just let things be as they are. With no desire, aren't you free? That is the essence and the pathway to *Mushin.* Let go.

Finding No Mind is as easy as letting go of your Known Mind.

Ravishing Zen Filmmaking
29/Nov/2022 11:26 PM

"We decided to try to play the algorithm game a little bit. Our videos haven't been finding much in the way of a new audience for quite a while, so we're changing up the title format for a bit to see if that helps reach new people. The old naming format with episode number can be found in the video description. PS For what it's worth the title change seems to be helping a bit, as this video is outperforming all of our recent videos by close to 20% so far."

This is a statement that a couple of, *"Content Creators,"* or whatever you want to call them put up in the comment section on YouTube about a piece that they created ripping on one of the films Donald G. Jackson and I created, Witch's Brew. The title of their presentation, *"What is "ZEN FILMMAKING" and why is it a TERRIBLE way to make movies?"* …So, they are making money by soiling the name of *Zen Filmmaking.* Is that right?

In terms of the movie they are discussing, I can't say that it was really a Zen Film in that it actually had a large portion of it written by a very established screenwriter who was a long-time friend of Don. But, it was a film created, in tandem, by my *Zen Filmmaking* Brother and I, so I call it a Zen Film.

And, just like I say about all film critics, if they love the craft of filmmaking so much and they have such a vast knowledge about filmmaking why aren't they out there making movies instead of critiquing the works of the people who do actual create films?

Anyway… Here's what I said to those content creators in a message,

Hey Guys,

Just got pointed to your new piece on ZF and Witch's Brew. Skimmed through it, seems pretty funny. Like the piece you did on RB7 way back when, you do get some stuff wrong. You should ask me. I'm an easy guy to get into contact with. Fact: Most of Witch's Brew was script based.

But, to the point... Zen Filmmaking is a Registered Trademark. I let most stuff go but you guy using it has already sent a lot of hate stuff my direction. Some people just want something or someone to be mad at. I don't want to do that YouTube Trademark take down thing as you guys seem like you're trying to put out a good product. You can love or hate my films, I don't care about any of that, you can even get your facts wrong, but you can't use Zen Filmmaking just to get yourself some more people if it's going to cause me grief. You know that's not the right thing to do.

Feel free to give me a shout next time you want to know something about a Zen Film.

All the best,
S.

You know, I always like to play nice. I always like to give the benefit of the doubt. But, here are these two guys, stealing footage from and making money off of ripping on a movie that holds U.S. Copyright and doing it intentionally. Not to mention their aforementioned statement where they clearly want to make money off of a Registered Trademark, *Zen Filmmaking,* just because they can. But, can they?

Now, it would only take me filling out the Trademark Form on YouTube and it would be pulled down, at least with that title. That is something I may have to do. But, I hate to do all that. For what does it equal? A push for a bunch of attacks on Scott Shaw for standing up for his rights of copyright and trademark which should be respected anyway.

Every time, including this time, one of these pieces is put out there I get tons of hate mail and threats. Do I want to ask for more? I mean, what is wrong with people?

I shouldn't have to do any of this! People should be honorable enough to not rip other people off. And, the copyright law is clear, take anybody's anything and make money from it and, *"Fair use,"* goes out the window. It becomes copyright infringement.

But, here we are. Here I am. Once again dealing with people ripping me off to make money. It shouldn't be this way. All of you people out there, who read this blog, should be telling them that they are wrong. But, what are you doing?

You see, this is the strange part about spirituality—about you people who read this blog. …And, there are a lot of you. You sit back in the cut. You let things go. You avoid all that life-stuff nonsense. And, I get it. Who wants to deal? Who wants to put themselves on the line?

I even noticed that one of the people who invites me to his movie showings and DM's me asking questions about my films, chiming right in on the comments. Did he say anything nice? Nope. Equal: Unfollow! Why do I want to have any association with anyone who will not stand up for me? …A person who does not understand what I am about and why I do what I do?

Me, I stand up for anyone who is good, trying to do good, and is in the right!

As stated in the statement to those two content creators, this is not about loving or hating the film. That's not the point. I don't care about that. What this is about is honor. People not intentionally ripping other people off to make a buck. People not creating a negative focus when there needs to be none. BE POSITIVE! That is my moto.

Love or hate a film, that is personal choice. But, doing nothing to stand up to the people who denigrate the artist that is something else altogether.

As all you people who know, know, *Zen Filmmaking* is about bringing artistic freedom and spiritual awareness to the filmmaking process. It is never about judgement for that is one of the lowest levels of human consciousness.

Is their presentation funny or interesting or ??? I guess it is if you want to watch two people being critical of other people and their artform. But, being on the other side of it, all I hear is spewing a false narrative with incorrect facts and not understanding what actually took place. I mean, how would they like it if I went through their footage and took a piece of their dialogues here, a piece there, put it together using their Brand name, and criticized how they looked or what they said while expounding false facts about them? Think about it... Is that right?

It always surprises me that I am contacted all the time by people liking what I do. In fact, someone claiming to like what I do told me about this piece on YouTube. But, what do they do? Do they ever go toe-to-toe with the haters, the intellectual property thieves? No, I never see them saying anything.

The other interesting thing, at least I find it interesting, is that people always go after Zen Films that were done twenty or thirty years ago. This one in question was predominately filmed in 1998. I haven't made a narrative film in over a decade. There's been no dialogue in my Zen Films, and I've made a lot of them, in something like fifteen years. *Zen Filmmaking* evolved to a more natural state solely based upon interlocking visual images; *The Non-Narrative Zen Films.* Few critics discus those films, however. I guess that's because they can't throw harsh criticism at the actors or the storyline, because there is none.

So, here's my comment for the day... And, I kind of say this all the time. Be Positive. If you encounter negativity, countermand it with positivity. I mean, how much effort does it take to stop the flow of negativity, (and theft). Get up off your butt and do something that may change the direction of the conversation. Not just in this situation, but in all situations. Even if the negativity is too deep, and you can't change it, at least if you tried and you can claim, *"I tried to turn the tide. I attempted to make things right. I added positivity to a negative situation."*

Be Honorable. Be Positive.

Post Script:

We're a couple of days into this event and I was just informed that the guys who did that presentation, heard me, and changed the title. I think that's nice. Thanks!

With those actions, I was going to take this piece down but then I thought that it does have a couple of points in it that I would like to get out there. So, I'll leave it up for now.

I believe there is an important lesson to learn in this for all of us. If someone tells you that they take offense at what you are doing or what you are saying or that what you are doing is hurting them, it is essential to hear them, listen to them, and change your behavior. Because if you don't, what does that make you?

*   *   *
29/Nov/2022 02:19 PM

Does saying something negative make you feel positive?

If it does, you should ask yourself why?

The Spoken Word
29/Nov/2022 06:52 AM

In the realm of poetry, it seems that people/the authors have been speaking their mind since time immemorial. They compose and put words together, in some abstract manner, forming a cohesion unity of what they hope to express. But, think of all the poets throughout time, how many people have ever read or heard their words? Most were scribble on a page and then lost to the hands of time. Where did those words go?

How about you, have you composed poetry that no one ever read?

There have been time periods, in modern history, when poetic words find a more interested public. Certainly, the 1950s into the 1960s was a time when poetry was embraced. But again, how many poets had their words heard? Very few in comparison to how many words were written (or spoken).

One of the trends that arose in that era was that people wrote their poetry, read it at a gathering, and then destroyed it. There must have been something very artistically freeing in that process. To create, share, experience, and then release. But, on the other side of this issue, then all that was created was lost.

Nearing the later part of the 1980s, *"Spoken word,"* sessions began to once again rise. Gatherings where people would speak their words/expound their truth. Like poetry, or because of poetry, words began to be a tool presented in whatever abstract manner the composer envisioned. But, who do words actually matter to? Do they matter only the poet? To the people who want to hear the words a specific individual speaks? Or everyone? ...Complicated question. ...Complicated answer.

Think about yourself. Do you read poetry? Have you ever read poetry? Do you care about poetry? If you do enjoy poetry, do you enjoy all poetry or only poetry written in a specific manner or by a specific person? Truthfully, do you like to listen to the words spoken by other people?

As I mentioned to you in this blog a little while back, one of my close friends, of over fifty years, passed away recently. I went to his funeral a couple of weeks ago. As the funeral approached, I became so worried that they were going to ask me to go up and speak about the man and our friendship. It truly worried me, because I felt I had nothing to say.

The funeral day arrived. It got underway. A couple of people voluntary spoke, one even referencing me as the man's best friend. Then, it was the time when then mic was to be passed around by minister, asking did anyone want to say anything? The man's daughter, my goddaughter, looked at me, I could tell she wanted me to say something, but I didn't know what to say. Years-upon-years, decades-upon-decades of knowing the man but what could I say? Thankfully, I was allowed to remain silent.

A day or so later, I was taking an afternoon walk and the strangest thing happened to me, it all came to me, I knew exactly what to say, or what I should have said. It was a very strange experience; the words, the situations to speak of, whom to reference, it all came to me. But, there was no one to say those words to; only me.

For the next couple of days those words reverberated in my head. I questioned what to do with them but there was nothing. The time was gone when they could have been spoken.

Then, I thought to those who destroyed their poetry after it was written. I thought to all that poetry that was written but never read by anyone. I thought of the Akashic Record were all things thought, done, lived, and unlived are recorded for eternity, and I realized that perhaps the not saying anything and the not doing anything with those lately discovered words was the perfect form of Zen. Known but unknown. Thought but experienced by no one. Lived but unlived. All this, equaling the perfect expression of Satori.

Reality is an Illusion
28/Nov/2022 08:44 AM

Recently, I finally got around to watching the film, *Don't Worry Darling,* plus I just finished up the Netflix series, 1899. Not to give too much away, but they are both based in people living in a simulated reality but not knowing it until the end. I knew it was coming. I was hoping it wasn't. But, I could just feel it from very early on in the theatrical presentations that was what was going to happen.

Though the concept of living in an artificial reality may be relatively new, this idea and this ideology has been going on forever. In Hinduism, the concept of, *"Maya,"* is based in this same understanding; that all reality is an illusion.

Since the birth of the Hindu writings, thousands of years ago, they have been discussing this subject. This concept moved onto Buddhism and onwards from there.

Remember, and this is something most people may not even care to realize, just like Jesus was a Jew, the Buddha was a Hindu. Thus, all Buddhists are Hindus, and all Christians are Jews.

This being said, there is life and then there is life. Meaning, most people live their life from a very sterile and basic perspective. They see what they see, feel what they feel, want what they want, but they observe, think, or experience nothing beyond the obvious.

From the dawn of rising consciousness, there have been those who have sought beyond the obvious. They seek to know the wisdom of the absolute truth of life. For some of these people they concluded the fact that the observable life we live and feel is all illusionary. That there is something more beyond the seen. For them, at least some of them, they claim that all life is Maya; illusion. From this belief there have been many precepts put out to the world about the various way this illusion may occur.

Now, this is an arguable point, for some would argue that if it is not obvious than it is not real, while others, (including myself), would claim, the greatest illusion is that there is no illusion at all. But, I do not believe that there is any person that has not felt that there is something in the Out There that is unknown and unseen. Most just simply acknowledge this fact and move on through their life giving it very little thought. Or, they cast it all to religion: that is god, that is god's way, that is my guardian angel, and all the stuff like that.

At the heart of enlightenment, however, there is the need to know. There is the necessity for personal realization. For those who walk this path, they are the ones who delve deeply into the question of life as an illusionary projection. But, then what? What is their ultimate conclusion? What is the ultimate conclusion? Though they may find their own personal realization of having transcended the Mind of No Mind to the degree where they may be able to express their belief to a large portion of other people, have those other people been able to follow that individual's path and come to the same realization? No. At best/at most they found their own truth in the abstract realms of this consciousness and though they may have told others about their realization, few if any, had the same realization. Why? Because realization is an individual process. There is no mass realization. There is only self-realization.

In today's reality, yes, you can dive deep into your computer monitor, you can put on eye goggles and headphones and become lost in your game's world. But, is that an alternate reality? Some would claim, *"Yes, it is."* But, the denial factor in this is that you must come out at some point. You must take off your goggles, your headset, or turn off your computer. What are you left with then? Answer: Known reality. So, what you were doing/where you were living was not real.

Since the advent of advancing human consciousness, some pundits have claimed known reality is not the ultimate reality. It has been spoken about in scriptures, novels, and now portrayed in movies. But, all this is simply a ploy to cast doubt and set people on a course where there is no absolute or final end goal. Just like in the two aforementioned theatrical presentations, the central characters were forced into an alternate reality where they struggled to find their way out only to ultimately realize that all they wanted was to get back to the level of common and accepted reality that they previously lived.

Seeking the truth of truth, the reality of reality, is the highest goal any of us can hope to achieve. Being forced to play a game we don't want to play, being force to lived someone else's conjured up supposed reality, defined by someone else who believes that they know what is best for us, is nothing more than imprisonment. Being lured into believing that there is something there that is not, is simply someone trying to pretend that they know more than you can ever know. Setting you on a pathway of spending your entire life seeking to find a glitch in the reality your living is nothing more than looking for a pathway to developed insanity.

No matter what anyone says, no matter what anyone claims is out there, this is the reality you, I, and everyone was handed. If it is a false reality, why do we all experience it in the same manner?

Instead of seeking to find a way out, seek to find a way in. A place where you can be the perfect example of yourself and where you live all you see and experience from the most pure and thought-full place possible.

You want the truth of absolute reality, you are already living it.

Not Knowing What You Don't Know
27/Nov/2022 07:58 AM

Zen is a pathway of loss. You lose what you already don't have.

What don't you have? You see this is the question that most people never ask themselves, which is what sets the followers of Zen apart from the rest of humanity.

I am certain you can tell me what you do have. I am certain you can tell me what you want. But, can you tell me what you don't have?

Here's the question, what don't you have?

Answer, you cannot know the answer to that question because if you don't know what you don't have you can never claim not to have it.

Yes, this is a paradox. But, paradox is what Zen is based upon.

Think about all of the things you believe you know. Think about all of the things you own. Think about all of the relationships you have. Those are all the known.

But now, think about this, how many times has something you owned become broken? Did you expect that? Did you know that was going to happen?

How many times has something you own become stolen? Did you expect that? Did you know that was going to happen?

How many times have you thought a person was one thing but they turned out to be another. How many times did someone you know do something to you didn't like? Did you expect that? Did you know that was going to happen?

What this tells us is that even the known is unknown because you can never know what is going to happen next. That is the reality of life that most people try to hide from.

All that is known is known, but is it? What about what is unknown?

Think about this, what don't you know? I am sure a list of things that you don't know may come to mind. But, how superficial is that list? Isn't that list just made of things that are already in your mind?

Here's the reality, all those things are known. You know you don't know them. That means that you do know them. What about all of those things that you have no idea about—never heard of—never contemplated. That is what you don't know.

Most people spend their entire life based in a reality of what they believe they know. Even if they don't know how to do something or how to get something or how to operate something, they know about it. From this, though new learning may be gained, it is all based in the already known. That is not Zen.

Zen is based in the fact that you can't know what you don't know. Zen is based in the fact that because you don't know, you can never know. As long as you believe you know, what is known is not the true expression of Zen, thus nirvana cannot be experienced.

Zen is understanding you can never really know. Zen is finding the space where all is unknown. By embracing this reality, the unknown became the conduit for the realization of No Mind. No Mind is the essence of Zen for in that not knowing anything, and knowing you don't know anything, pure realization can be found.

When You Try to Help but Fail
26/Nov/2022 07:48 AM

For some of us, we set about on a life course where we intentionally try to help people, to the best of our ability, throughout all life situations. There are others who try to help people when a situation presents itself. And yes, there are those who do not try to help at all but intentionally try to hurt, break things, upset, injure, offend other people, and do all that kind of stuff that we all know, deep down, is just wrong. Which one are you?

Have you ever had one of those situations happen to you where you are trying to help someone but it goes the other way—your help turns into a not-help? What then? Were your intentions wrong? Was your presentation of the help wrong? Was your attempting to help in the first place wrong? Or, (maybe), was the person on the receiving end of the help wrong?

Have you ever met one of those people who expects help from everyone? They just can't do anything, so they are always looking to someone else to do their stuff for them. Is helping a person like that actually providing help?

Of course, you could argue that point. And, there are two ways to look at it. But, the larger question must be asked, are you here/there to help or not? If you are, is helping always helping?

Have you even tried to help someone in some physical manner? …Do some physical action for them. But, your help turned into hurt. You didn't mean for that to happen. You didn't want that to happen. But, it happened, now what? Do you help to fix your previous help that turned out badly? Do you just turn and walk away? Is the other person now mad at you that they accepted your help? Again, now what? What do you do?

Have you ever had someone seem lost in their life? …Someone who maybe even admittedly is defined by some missing life element. They question their life to you. Maybe they even ask for your advice. But, when you give it to them, they do not like your response. Maybe it makes them sad, angry, hurt or whatever. Were you helping them by telling them your ideas? Was it your fault they did not like your response? Or, was it theirs? Post all of this occurring, were you actually helping them or were you hurting?

Some people in their helping attempt to position themselves as the helper. They want the credit for having done what they have done. They want their help to cause others to feel good about them. And, they want their help to make them feel good about themselves. Is that you? If it is, is that help at all?

On the other side of this, when you help, do you help from a pure space of hoping to actually make things better and that is your only motivation? Or, are you locked somewhere between the two?

Help is a complicated subject. Some people don't want your help. Some people are forced into accepting your help. Some people suck all of the help energy they can from everyone they can. But, keep in mind, however your help energy arrives: be it physical, mental, monetary, or whatever, by you helping you have stepped into another person's karma. You have entered a field that you did not create. By doing this, all of your actions, no matter how well-meaning, will have consequences. Hopefully they will all be positive but that is not always the case.

Remember by helping you create an entirely new world of possibility, both good and bad. Who are you going to help next. Why? And, what consequences will your helping actually create?

Max Hell Frog Warrior: The History and The Evolution
25/Nov/2022 11:41 AM

Here's a chapter from the book, *Donald G. Jackson: Soldier of Cinema* that those of you interested in the movie, *Max Hell Frog Warrior* may find interesting.

The film, *Max Hell Frog Warrior* has an interesting set of circumstance that set its creations into motion. Certainly, its evolution goes back to the cult film classic, *Hell Come to Frogtown.* From there, Donald G. Jackson and Scott Shaw set about creating an entirely new interpretation of its foundation.

Frogtown is a geographic region of Los Angeles, California that skirts the Los Angeles River. It first gained this name when it was overrun with frogs in the 1930s. A friend of Donald G. Jackson's, Sam Mann, lived in this area. As the story goes, one day the two men were driving around discussing movie ideas and Mann came up with the title, *Hell Comes to Frogtown.* As he had already starred in Jackson's films, *Roller Blade* and *Roller Blade Warriors,* he was the obvious choice to perform the roll of Sam Hell, the lead character of the film. There was a screenplay written for this film by Donald G. Jackson's friend and writing collaborator, Randal Franks. It was titled, *The Adventures of Sam Hell.*

Jackson initially planned to finance the movie with his credit cards as he had done with his film, *Roller Blade.* In the interim, however, he had become involved with New World Pictures. They liked the concept and they offered to finance it for him. The only problem was, he had to add a completely different cast than was his intention. His actor/friends were to be replaced by, *"Name Actors."* Sam Mann, the actual inspiration for Sam Hell, was to be replaced by the then very famous wrestler, Rowdy Roddy Piper. Don asked Sam for his approval, which he gave.

Until his dying day, Donald G. Jackson regretted this decision. He was not only sorry that Mann had been replaced but the movie was eventually taken away from his creative control and it lost much of the visual landscaped he had hoped to create with it.

Approximately five years after *Hell Comes to Frogtown* was released; Don had formed a filmmaking alliance with Tanya York. She had a financier in place that was willing to bankroll her first feature films as an executive producer. As she had a longstanding relationship with Jackson, the two moved forward and created Frogtown II. For Jackson, the only problem was, again, much of the creative control was taken away from him. Ultimately, he again, was left with a film that he did not like.

During this same period, just after the completion of *Frogtown II,* York wanted to finance another Jackson film. He offered up his Roller Blade series. The 1991/1992 outcome was the first and second Zen Films, *The Roller Blade Seven* and *Return of the Roller Blade Seven,* created by Donald G. Jackson and Scott Shaw.

After the completion of those two films, Shaw took the foundations for the *Zen Filmmaking* concept he had originated and went off on his own and immediately created, *Samurai Vampire Bikers from Hell* and several other films. Jackson also moved forward to create several script-based feature films.

In 1995, Shaw was in Thailand. Jackson contacted him to reconnect and make another feature film. When Shaw returned, the two set about creating the next Jackson/Shaw Zen Film.

Initially, the team toyed with the idea of creating a humorous filmed based on Jackson's, *Hell Comes to Frogtown* theme, titled, *Road Toad.* This film was to star Scott Shaw and co-star Julie Strain. The team eventually discarded this concept and then set about on the idea of, *Hell Comes to Hog Town.* This film was to be based on the artistic intent of the film, *Zachariah,* the First Electric Western, which starred a young Don Johnson. This film would have Shaw ridding in, (with an electric guitar strapped over his shoulder), on his 1966, bright yellow, Harley Davidson, Electra-Glide. He would then battle the forces of evil that were controlled by an evil warlord known as, The Hog, to be played by Joe Estevez. But, eventually this storyline was also put to rest.

What emerged from this period of creative interaction was Jackson's desire to do the story he had hoped to present with the original, *Hell Comes to Frogtown*—the story of a frog plague unleashed on the earth by an evil overseer who would eventually be destroyed by the antihero. Enter, *Toad Warrior.*

Toad Warrior AKA *Hell Comes to Frogtown III* went up in the winter of 1996 on a shoestring budget. In association with Jackson as the Producer/Director, Shaw was to perform the lead role as well as Co-Produce and Co-Direct the film. The team of Jackson and Shaw brought on their friend and frequent collaborator, Joe Estevez, to play the bad guy. They also brought on Jill Kelly, who had her first on-screen appearance in the *Roller Blade Seven,* and had since gone on to become a major force in the adult film industry. In addition, the team brought into the production: Selina Jayne and Roger Ellis — both of whom had appeared in the *Roller Blade Seven* and had gone on to co-star in Shaw's, *Samurai Vampire Bikers from Hell* and *Samurai Johnny Frankenstein.*

Jackson and Shaw filmed, *Toad Warrior* in the high desert of California and various other locations throughout Hollywood, Los Angeles, and at their production offices in North Hollywood. Quickly, the production began to express and represent all the aspects of the bizarre *Zen Filmmaking* minds of the Jackson/Shaw team.

When production was complete on *Toad Warrior*, the team quickly moved forward onto other filmmaking projects. The next on the production schedule was *Shotgun Blvd.*, AKA, *Armageddon Blvd.*, immediately followed by *Ghost Taxi*, AKA, *Ride with Devil*.

As the 1997 American Film Market was quickly approaching, the production team of Jackson/Shaw knew that they had to compete several projects. Shaw took on the role of editor for *Armageddon Blvd.* and *Ride with the Devil*, while they turned *Toad Warrior* over to a longtime friend of Jackson—the editor of a number of his films, Christopher Blade.

The 1997 American Film Market premiered several Jackson/Shaw films. They included the one's named above and a thirty minute, long-form trailer, of a film they had not yet completed, *Guns of El Chupacabra*.

Though the Jackson/Shaw team was happy to have Toad Warrior edited and available, it was never the film that they had hoped to make. Though the needed footage and scenes were all there, they were not constructed in a manner the filmmakers had hoped.

At the 1997 American Film Market buyers from Japan, Malaysia, and the Philippines purchased the rights to release *Toad Warrior* theatrically and show it in movie theaters. Shaw attended the Tokyo premiere of the film. Jackson and Shaw held back on U.S. sales, however, as they wanted to reedit the movie.

The following few years proved to be a very busy time for the filmmaking team of Jackson/Shaw. Though they had hoped to get back to the film *Toad Warrior* and re-edited it, this never came to pass. Shaw did, however, condense the originally edited footage of the film into what the team called, a Zen Speed Flick, and released it with the title, *Max Hell in Frogtown*.

By the early part of the twenty-first century, Jackson had become very ill from his battle with leukemia. He passed away in 2003. Soon after this, a distribution company somehow came upon a beta master of the film, *Toad Warrior,* and released it in a compilation DVD. Let alone the fact that Jackson/Shaw never wanted this version of the film released in the West, many of the titles and screen credits of this version were incorrect.

Due to copyright infringements, this DVD was eventually removed from the market. By this point in time, Shaw had already revamped the film and had released it as, *Max Hell Frog Warrior.*

As the unauthorized bootlegged version of the film had already been released, Shaw decided it was best to release an authorized version of *Toad Warrior* in order to help in countermanding any further unlawful distribution of the film's unauthorized version. He did this in 2007.

As of 2012, Shaw still plans to go back into the original footage of the film, reedit it, and create the film that Jackson and he had initially hoped for.

In recent years, there has been an ongoing interest in the film. Similar to the Jackson/Shaw creation of, *The Roller Blade Seven, Max Hell Frog Warrior* has continued to draw interest from critics and cult movie aficionados. So much so, that the writers of the HBO television series, *Newsroom,* mentioned *Max Hell* in an episode of their show broadcast in August of 2012.

Growing from the minds of Sam Mann, Donald G. Jackson, and Scott Shaw, the Frogtown series shows no signs of being forgotten in the near future.

* * *
24/Nov/2022 07:10 AM

If I tell a joke that I think is funny, but you don't find funny, who is right?

The Way You Want Someone to Behave
23/Nov/2022 08:46 AM

Have you ever encountered one of those people who expects you to behave in a certain manner and when you do not they get mad at you? They want you to give them what they want. They expect you to provide them with the answers they want to hear with the words they want them spoken in. They want you to behave in the manner that they want you to behave.

It always surprises me when I encounter someone like this. …Though I suppose it shouldn't. People like that are all over the place. Of course, we all try to steer clear of this type of person, but sometimes they find their way into our life.

For some, due to their profession, they must deal with people all the time. For them, encountering un-nice people is a more frequent occurrence than for those of us who do not work in the public sector. An individual living this lifestyle must learn how to cope with that style of Behavior Expectant people, because, if they cannot learn how to deal, their entire life and Life Time will be haunted by the expectations thrown upon them by others.

Most of us are not like that, however. We are not forced to deal with people on a day-to-day basis. Even though this is the case, sometime, we too, are confronted with that style of person forcing their way into our sphere of existence.

Think about a time when one of these people came knocking at your door. How did they find you? Were they searching you out, expecting to get what they wanted from you? Or, did you nonchalantly let them in, not knowing what you had opened yourself up to?

In either case, once they were at your door, expecting you behave in the manner they desired, they unleashed the fact that they wanted you to give them what they wanted, in whatever form they desired it. I am sure this made your life miserable. I know those situations, when they have occurred to me, have made me lose my peace and be unhappy.

What did you do? How did you deal with the situation?

The reason I ask this question is because how you answer it sets the standard for your life. For example, did you hold firmly to your ground and not shift your attitude or behavior for that person in any manner? Or, did you give into their whims?

The thing is, people who behave in this fashion are oftentimes very authoritarian. If you are different from what they want or expect, if you do not behave in the manner they deem appropriate, then they will often times become very hurtful and/or heavy-handed in their actions and reactions to you. Many of the people take to personal or psychological attacks, some even become physical.

All of this wrong! It is simply them being of such a low mind that they cannot let a person simply be who they are. But, this fact does not stop them.

All across the world you see people being judgmental of other people. Isn't this the same thing as someone expecting a person to behave in a specific manner? They want what they want out of that person and when they do not get it, they criticize them.

Of course, that is the early and rudimentary stages of this style of behavior. But, it happens all the time. Think about yourself. Analyze how you react towards others. What do you say and what do you do when someone does something that you do not agree with? How do you behave towards a person who does not give you what you want or hope to receive from them?

As I say over-and-over again, all life begins with you. What you do and how you treat others sets an entire plethora of actions, reactions, and karma into motion.

Okay... There is someone in your life expecting you to behave the way they want you to behave. What do you do when that is not the way you act? What do you do when behaving in that manner goes against everything that you are and everything that you believe? If you give in, who are you? If you don't give in, what are the consequence?

You see, this is where life, and dealing with this style of a person, gets complicated. Sometimes you can just blow them off. Other times, however, if you do, they will go on the attack and attempt to hurt you or your life. That's not right, but that is sometimes how this style of person behaves.

I wish I could provide you with an absolute answer to the problem of dealing with a person who possesses this mindset. But, each situation is so different. For me, I always give someone a chance to realize their folly and to stop behaving badly with their enhanced expectations towards me. In other words, I hope for the best.

Some people, when they are alerted to how they are behaving, can change their course. They care enough to care about someone else, at least to the degree that they stop expounding their expectations onto that individual and/or stop expecting or demanding things from their life. Others are simply selfish individuals. They want what they want and that is the end of their story. I say, get that type of a person out of your life as quickly as possible. I get it, in some cases that is not easy. But, the best defense against any form of negativity is positivity. Be the GOOD person. Be the BETTER person. Never let anyone define who you should be, what you should do, or how you should behave, especially when that outside person is only in it to get what they want out of you. As long as what you are saying and doing is good, helpful, positive, and non-demanding, why should you change your anything for anybody else?

In-Considerate
22/Nov/2022 10:35 AM

Have you ever had somebody do something really inconsiderate to you? I'm sure you have. We all have. ...Something that really messes with a moment (or longer) of your life. Don't you hate that?

Some inconsiderate things are done intentionally. Those are the worst. The person knows what they are doing, and they do it to do it anyway, consciously knowing that it will negatively affect you and/or your life.

Other people are inconsiderate, but they do it unknowingly. In some ways (I guess) that is forgivable. ...Depending on the circumstance. But, them not calculation or understanding what they are doing does not make it any less life debilitating.

There's the small situations of inconsiderate behavior. Those passing moments, that just pass by. But, in those passing moments, they can be quite annoying.

Yesterday, I was driving and I was in one of those left turn lanes waiting on the left arrow light. It was at one of those intersection where it takes a long time for the light to change. Anyway, the left arrow comes on but none of the cars in front of me move. I give a little beep on my horn as maybe the front car is messing around on their phone or something. Nothing, no movement. Finally, I see that a guy is walking very slowly across the street against a red light. When he finally passes, the two cars in front of me jam through the intersection against a yellow then red light. Me, I'm stuck waiting for the long light to change again.

I look over at the guy, slow walking. He was just your very average white guy. Very clean cut and his clothing was clean. He was wearing a clean tee-shirt, shorts, a baseball cap, and carrying a backpack. To see him, under any other circumstance, you would never take any notice. Then, I notice that he begins talking to himself and making subtle but weird hand gestures. So, maybe he is high, maybe he is mentally ill, maybe he is on the spectrum, maybe??? But, due to who he is and the choice he made, what he did was inconsiderate.

Who's to blame? Him for not caring about the affect he is having on others or me for being impatient?

Today, I was driving home from breakfast. I have to turn right up at this one street but the car in front of me was going very-very slow and riding their breaks their entire way. Frustrating… When they finally turn, they come to a complete stop mid turn. I could see the driver, an elderly lady, was trying to figure out where to go and/or how to get there. Dead stopped in the street, cars cueing up behind me. What was she thinking? Who was she thinking about? Anybody but herself? No. Equaling, inconsiderate.

…If you're too old drive, you really shouldn't drive.

Those are two very small examples in the grand spectrum of life. But, they clearly illustrate the how being inconsiderate is based upon one person thinking only about themselves.

It's easy to find a time in your memory banks when someone was inconsiderate to you. But, take a moment right now and think about a time when you were inconsiderate to someone else. Really chart that moment out.

Now, here's the problem in this… As being inconsiderate is based in a selfish act, you thinking about nothing but your own space of reality, do you even know all of the times you have been inconsiderate? Do you even know all of the damage you created by you being inconsiderate? Maybe the person or persons did not tell you. Maybe you were so lost in your own mind that you did not even know or notice what you had done.

Isn't that the true definition of being inconsiderate? You only thinking of you.

But, back to the fact… Chart out a time that you did some inconsiderate something to someone. Who was it?

Why was it? What motivated you to do it? Would you do it again? But, most importantly, what did you do after the fact? Did you apologize? Did you try to right your inconsiderate wrong? Or, as most inconsiderate people do, did you just dismiss that other person's displeasure about what you did?

All life is based upon life interaction. What do your life interactions equal? Are they giving, caring, and thinking endeavors? Or, are they simply based in you thinking about you, equaling your inconsiderate actions?

Think about it? Who do you want to be? How do you want to be thought of and remembered? …As someone who cares about the all and the everyone else or someone who is just inconsiderate?

There Are No Secret Techniques
21/Nov/2022 07:23 AM

Ever since the martial arts found their way to the Western World there have been, *"Secret Techniques,"* that have been spoken about. Some Secret Something that only this ONE very specific individual knows and can teach. Some of these so-call Secret Techniques were shrouded in mystery. *"You can't learn it from the person until you have studied from them for years,"* and stuff like that.

Some people, some really good thespian, have even staged these elaborate demonstrations showing how they can do things like knock people down with simply them pointing their cosmic energy in a person's direction. Their students fly all over the place.

Have you ever seen one of those demonstrations in person or on TV? I had the privilege of being present for one of those. And me, being a Non-Believer, questioned it. *"Come up here, I will demonstrate." "Okay."* But, nothing. The supposed secret energy the man directed my direction did nothing. It was then detailed that because I did not believe it did not work. What? You have to believe in the con to be conned?

There have also been a lot of practitioners who claim secret knowledge about the pressure points and that they can simply touch an opponent and win any confrontation. Again, there have been numerous demonstrations demonstrating these supposed techniques.

And sure, there are pressure points on the human body that can, when impacted correctly, cause a lot of pain and stuff. Think about a time when you've accidentally bumped your funny bone and it hurts! That's what acupuncturists do. But, they are not claiming what they do is some secret knowledge, simply studied knowledge.

I met this one man claiming he had all this secret knowledge about how to disable his opponent's with just a touch. His students were falling left and right. *"Try it on me."* What he did was grab for a pressure point that any advanced martial artists knows about. All I did was shift my arm slightly and he had no effect.

It's not secret people! There's been books written about it, it's been taught in tons of classes on all of the continents, and the knowledge can be known if you look for it!

This is the same with spirituality, especially Eastern Spirituality. There is all of this promised mysticism and secret knowledge spoken of. All of this, *"You are too impure,"* to ever understand. Again, this is all someone feeding into the illusion of they know, or that person (their teacher) knows, and you do not. It is all about separation. The, *"I am more than you,"* mentality. But, anyone who proclaims this style of knowing is just lost in a lie. They are not being truthful to you, anyone else, and maybe even themselves.

Yes, someone may know something that you do not know. Yes, someone may know how to do something that you do not know how to do. But, that's what schools are for. That is the basis of the teacher, student relationship. Nothing is, *"Secret."* At most, it is unknown to you.

There are no Secret Techniques.

*   *   *
21/Nov/2022 06:25 AM

The News of Today is Not the News of Tomorrow.

*

*   *   *
20/Nov/2022 02:28 PM

Does a thief feel guilty about stealing?

No, or they would not steal.

Does a liar feel guilty about lying?

No, or they would not lie.

* * *

20/Nov/2022 02:28 PM

We all have had a yesterday.

* * *
20/Nov/2022 07:05 AM

You can't talk sense into a person who has no sense.

You Owe Me $35.00
19/Nov/2022 07:29 AM

    This afternoon, someone reminded me of this martial arts organization that used to be based out of the East Bay, near San Francisco, a number of years ago. Well, I guess they're still around, in some form, but they no longer hold and/or use the very established Korean organizational title that they once possessed. What happened, I have no idea??? But, them's the facts…

    Anyway… I was teaching a course at Cal., (University of California, Berkeley), in the later 1990s. I would fly up there each week to teach the class. On a number of occasions, I would drop by their studio, speak to the daughter of the president of the organization, who was very nice and forthcoming with the truth about a lot of the realities of what was going on in the Korean martial arts, both here and in Korea, at that time, and sometimes I would watch the classes that they taught. She was also the one who handled the organizational membership stuff.

    I met the president of the organization and stuff like that. Seemed like a good guy. He thought it was interesting that my 7th dan Korean Hapkido Federation ID Card had Australia on it, not the U.S. But, that's where I was practicing when I receive that rank advancement. I had never really thought that much about it…

    Anyway… On one of the later times I was there, the daughter suggested that I join their organization. Sure, I thought. Why not? Her father was one of the recognized first-generation Korean born masters, their association held one of the most established names there was in the Korean martial arts, and they operated the organization, actually based in Korea, from their studio in the East Bay. Meaning, they were so close. …Well, like five hundred miles from L.A. But, you know what I mean. Mostly, I would be able to easily communicate with them, which is something that was and still is not easy to do with the organizations based in South Korea.

When I got home, I filled out the form she gave me and sent in a check for the $35.00 membership fee. But then, nothing. I never heard from her again.

My teaching assignment was over, so I wasn't flying into SF each week. Well, I was actually flying into Oakland, as that airport is so much calmer than SFO. When I did go up there, it seemed no one was around at their studio. Time went on and I kind of forgot about the $35.00 and joining their organization. But, I was reminded of it today.

In the years following that, I heard from a number of people about them having problems with their membership, their certificates from the organization, and stuff. But, for someone like me, who has been around since the birth of the Korean martial arts in American, I knew this was nothing new and paid it little mind.

Time has gone on; decades, in fact. I don't really know what became of the man, (the president), his daughter, her brother who was teaching the classes, and the organization itself. I wonder if mismanagement had anything to do with their being removed from their prestigious place in the Korean organizational hierarchy? ...That's not throwing a shot or anything, because I truly liked everyone I met there very much. Just a question?

It's kind of a funny thing, I think... Organizations and all that... In my lifetime, even some of the biggest martial art organizations have come and gone. Then, what did their all-powerful, certified certificate issuance actually mean? The president of the biggest Taekwondo organization in the world actually did time for some of his wrong doings in getting Taekwondo into the Olympics. A million years ago, I met the man, had dinner with the man, seemed like a good guy. He even signed a couple of my certificates. So, what does that/this all mean? Like I have long believed, one-on-one teaching, learning, and certification is the best form of martial art advancement. You know the person. They know you. What better method of interpersonal knowledge is there than that? And, what does a piece of paper actually mean anyway? Pretty much anyone can print one now. I've known a lot of martial artists, who've claimed a whole lot of stuff, based on a piece of paper they possessed. But, were they actually making the world a better place or were they just riding their ego?

I don't know about you, but don't you hate it when someone sucks you in, takes your money, and then you end up with nothing? ...Nothing, except a blog like this.

Anyway... Just some thoughts and remembrances broadcast out to the world. But hey, you owe me $35.00! ☺

Great Minds Focus On What They Focus On
18/Nov/2022 09:25 AM

There certainly can be very little doubt that one of the greatest historians that ever lived on the subject of Buddhism was D.T. Suzuki; Daisetsu Teitaro Suzuki. His writings on the subject were voluminous and truly delved into all aspects of the topic. There can be little debate that his writings truly exposed the sublet nuisance of Buddhism to the Western world. To this day his writings are some of the most read and quoted materials on the subject. I can think of no other historian who provided such as service to the dissemination of Buddhism.

What was the greatest quality of this man's work? Answer: His focus. He was keenly focused on exploring and propagating a singular subject.

I won't provide you with his biography here, nor am I going to details his writings. All of this information is easily acquired. I will, however, suggest that you do investigate him and them. For the novice, the zealot, or the scholar of Buddhism, D.T. Suzuki is a fascinating source of information.

As questioned, what was the greatest quality of this man's work? Focus. He chose his subject and through a lifetime of dedicated research and practice he was able to literally spread the knowledge he gained out to the world.

This characteristic of acute focus is something that very few people possess. This, I believe, is why so few people can actually make a difference in whatever it is they focus their life upon. Whereas D.T. Suzuki focused his life on true research, most people just willy-nilly their way through their life. They like what they like, they believe what they believe, but they never travel to the source of any of that, nor do they truly investigate and grow in developing an actual understanding of the true essence of anything that they hold in their mind. It is just there with no sense of factual guarantee.

Think about your own life. How have you lived it? Yes, you undoubtedly have thought what you have thought, believed what you have believed, but where is your root consciousness?

Yes, you were taught to believe what you believe. Yes, you were schooled in how to believe it? But, why? Where is the source of anything you think and believe? Are you focused on traveling to the source of whatever that Mind Think is and actually finding out the factors that set that whatever into motion? Probably not. Most people do not choose to possess the dedication to truly focus and find out the reason, *"Why,"* of what they think.

If you don't know, you don't know.

People, especially people who base their lives around religion, commonly expound the statement, *"Just believe. That is what faith is."* And, various other proclamations like that. But, is that truth? No.

Others, those who climb onto the pulpit say, *"Believe me. I know."* But, what do they know? What is their truth?

Most people are somewhere lost in the middle, simply living their life, thinking what they think, and doing what they do. But, in all of that, where does the basis of their anything come from? Where is their essence? Where is their cause and case for being? Why are they doing what they do, if what they do has no directed purpose?

Most of us never will poses the singular mind and directed focus of a man like D.T. Suzuki. But, that does not mean that we cannot strive to become that someone with something more than simply a person who passes through their life driven by whims and the selfish knowledge developed by someone else, who seeks nothing more than to be in control of our minds. We can strive to seek the source of what we think and what we believe.

If we can each strive to enter a new and more developed level of knowledge and understanding, we can then claim we are the sourcepoint of the knowledge we hold. With this, not only do we become a more whole and complete individual but then, we may even be able to present our knowledge to others and the whole world with a basis in fact.

Choose to become something more than nothing more than a believer. Have the dedication to find your own truth-based facts.

Your Words Are What Gets You Into Trouble
18/Nov/2022 03:57 AM

I had to go to one of those soirees last night. It was on the far side of the city, and I had to take off for it at the height of L.A evening traffic. It was a horrendous two-hour drive.

It was a dinner event, held at a restaurant. That's fine. The food was good. But, what the event lead me to was once again realizing the lack of necessity for conversation. I mean, people talk about so much of nothing—they look to find something to talk about. But, what does any of that equal?

It always seems that someone seeks me out at these gatherings and wants to know what I do. First of all, I forever try to hide myself at these events. I do that just to avoid such a conversation. When forced into the conversation, *"A little bit of this and a little bit of that,"* is my common response. But, that doesn't usual fulfill the, *"Askers,"* questionnaire. Moreover, I'm always afraid of saying the wrong thing. People have such a propensity for misunderstanding and turning the words of other people around. Thus, I just prefer to say nothing.

I always come away from those events feeling a little dirty. …Worried that what I have said may be misunderstood or misinterpreted. That's why I try to say nothing.

Which brings me to the point of all of this. There was this guy sitting across the table from me. Seemed like a nice guy. He spoke about recently going and seeing a concert and stuff like that. But, as it turns out, he has had, what I would consider, an illustrious life. He was in the military where he learned to fly helicopters. After that, he went to work for the L.A.P.D. where he became a SWAT officer. Now, he flies helicopters for the police department and trains others in that field. Plus, one of his sons is studying at Annapolis Naval Academy. This guy has made a true contribution to society but said nothing about it. It was his mother-in-law who told me his story.

The thing about life is, there is all of these people spitting so much BS out there, trying to make a name for themselves by saying what they say. Whether it is on the various levels of social media platforms, in magazines, newspapers, blogs, vlogs, you name it… They talk to be heard. They want others to see them as some sort of an authority. But, they have done nothing with their life. Have they served their country? Have the served their community? Have they followed a pathway where they actually work to help and, in fact, save others? Have they set up a generational pathway where their children will do the same? The answer to all of these questions is, no. They just talk.

I believe that each of us really needs to step back and think about what we say and why we are saying it. Especially those of us who have not formally walked down the path of True Service. Because if all you are is someone telling others what you think about whatever it is you think about, truly what have you provided to the world?

The Things That No One Else Cares About
17/Nov/2022 01:33 PM

I came home this AM from my morning run, and I decided to put on an LP: Regina, Curiosity. I turned on the Marantz receiver. (Vintage, of course). I put on the LP, getting ready to have it playing as my background music but the needle slides across the record. *"What!"* I try it again and it starts to play but then keeps skipping. *"Damn it!"*

My turntable is an Audio-Technica AT-LP 120. The thing about this turntable, and turntables like it is, it has very advanced and complicated system of balancing the arm and the needle. It is one of those turntables that is set up for high-quality sound design.

Ever since I've owned it, and this has been for a number of years now, it was and is a very time-consuming process to set it up. But, once it is set up, the sound it produces is great. But, not today.

Now, I don't know what happened to it, 'cause it hasn't been moved or anything like that. But, something shifted its balance. So, there I stood, trying and trying to get it correctly set up once again, as it continued to slide across the record. Thankfully, I own another copy of that LP, 'cause my guess is that record is nowhere near in the perfect condition it was when I started this adventure.

So, there I was, FRUSTRATED. Dealing with the set-up, when all I wanted to do was play an LP. But, life and Life Stuff got in my way.

Here's the thing, do you care about any of this? Of course not. You could care less. You've got your own life stuff going on. Why would you care about mine?

This is the thing about All Reality; You care about You. Maybe you are happy. Maybe you are sad. Maybe, like I, you are frustrated. But, who cares? No one except maybe your closest amigos.

Most people don't understand this, however. When they are feeling whatever it is they are feeling, they think everyone should drop their All and their Everything and either feel happy for them feeling happy or fix whatever it is that is making them feel sad.

No one cares. That's the main thing you must remember in life. And, if they do, good for you. But, never bank on it. Because the minute something comes up in their life that is going to shift their attention, you and how you feel will be the farthest thing from their mind.

Think I may need to go and buy a new turntable.

Knowing Who You Know
17/Nov/2022 07:47 AM

In the long ago and the far-far away, people used to know who you are. You would meet someone, talk with someone, get to know someone, tell them about you, and they would tell you about them. From this, something was or was not created. At the root of that relationship was a relationship. But, times have changed…

Even with things like doctors, in the past you would get to know your doctor. I know I did. When I would walk into their office, they would know about me and what was going on with me. From there, they would be able to give me a better diagnosis. And, I knew about them and their life, as well.

There was one of my doctors, (nice guy), every now and then I would bump into him in a thrift store. I always thought that was very strange, a doctor, (someone at the top of the food chain), in a thrift store. But, like me, that is what he liked to do for a distraction. Sometimes when I would go to see him in his office, he would ask if I wanted to go, *"Junking,"* with him. That's what he called going to thrift stores. But no, some people would have loved that. But me, I tend to be a bit of a loner.

It's just like when I would bump into the GREAT actor Don Stroud around my neighborhood, before he moved back to Hawaii where he was originally from. He was always one of the actors I revered the most, from the 1960s forward. When I got to meet him on one of my first acting jobs, it was mind blowing. Then, to hang out and work with him on *Roller Blade Seven,* well, I felt I had arrived. He would invite me over to his place. A couple times I did show up, but I just couldn't do it. It was just all too weird for me. Hanging out with someone I considered so great. But, that's just me…

I'm getting off of the point here… But, maybe all that nonsense is to the point… People meet, they interact, they do or do not develop a relationship, and life moves on from there.

Now, though I suppose my doctor knows my face. But, he (or she), I have a couple, knowns nothing about me. They don't ask and I don't tell. I know nothing about them. Life has changed.

People out there, in the lost realms of cyberspace, claim to know something about me, but they have never met or spoken to me. How could they know anything?

I think this is where one of the biggest problems of current life arises, the not knowing what you think you know. I mean, we hear all the time about people being catfished online and stuff like that. But, even down to the more rudimentary level, think of all the people you think you On-Line know... Who are they really? What lie are they projecting? Who and what are they pretending to be?

Everybody is who they are. But, even in the life of real life, how many people project a false reality about who and what they truly are? How many people lie? How many people are lost in the realms of psychological fuck-up to the degree that they may even personally believe the lie they are projecting? Even more than that, how many people are just trying to GET? Get what they want by any means possible? If they do this in real life, and it has been done for eons, why do you think they are not doing it to you when you cannot even look them in the eyes?

True life, true relationships comes down to true interpersonal interactions. What interactions are you truly having? What interactions are you allowing to be had? Who do you meet? Who do you truly know? And, how much of your life is lived lost in the fabrication of not truly knowing who and what you are actually interacting with?

Racial Insensitivity
16/Nov/2022 09:17 AM

I was flipping channels last night and I came upon *Saturday Night Fever*. It's currently in rotation on one of the major power movie platforms. *Saturday Night Fever* is one of those really good movies that though you may have seen it many times, you can watch a little bit of it here or there just for a moment of distraction. …At least I can.

As I started watching it, I had come in on one of the parts where the characters were throwing a lot of very racially derogatory statements. I looked over at my lady and said, *"You could never make a movie like this today."*

That's the thing, I think times have changed and at least the evolved of society have progressed. They no longer use racially derogatory terms like were commonly used just a few years back.

I know I've referenced this way too many times, but when I grew up, being the only white kid in my grammar school, every day of the week I was called, *"Honky,"* or *"White Paddy,"* That derogatory labeling didn't really bother me that much. I just felt it was a sign of the time. But, I guess, it got so bad that one of my teachers, an African-American lady, Mrs. Larson, told the class that they really needed to stop it. Most tried, some did not. But, that kind of racially explicit language went on everywhere at that point in history, on all sides of the spectrum.

Speaking of movies, I think to this very good Colin Farrell and Salma Hayek film, *"Ask the Dust."* In it, Collin Farrell's character directs a lot of racial insensitive comments towards her. Nearing the end of the film, he apologizes, saying in essence, that is just what he grew up hearing and that is how he learned how to behave. I believe that's true with all of us. We learn what we learn from experience. And, from that, we mimic what we have heard and learned shaping how we treat and speak to and about others.

The thing is, we can each choose to be more than our programming. We can rise above how we were treated and what we learned from the way others behaved towards us and spoke to us. We can be more than our lessor counterparts and we can become more than our lessor self.

I am certain that all of us have made racial insensitive comments, whether knowingly or not, at some point in our life. I know I have heard them, in any number of languages, all across the globe. If an individual is not intentionally being racially insensitive, I guess we can forgive them. On the other hand, if they (if you) are saying those racist things intentionally, we need to separate ourselves from that person as we do not want to be defined by their unenlightened profiling.

Seeing a person for who they are, not what they are, is one of the greatest gifts you can give anyone. Allowing a person to Be and to Become not defined by what color of skin they were born into allows the all and the everyone to be a true and pure example of what they have to give to the world.

Don't define or judge a person by what color of skin they wear. Define them by what they say and what they do.

* * *

16/Nov/2022 08:51 AM

Not revealing the truth about what you are doing is the same thing as lying.

* * *
15/Nov/2022 11:54 AM

Next time you're having a bad day, think about a time when you were having a good day and someone else was having a bad day. Did you care about what they were experiencing?

When People Just Won't Listen
15/Nov/2022 09:00 AM

Have you ever tried to explain something to someone—something that you understand to be true, valid, just, and right but they will not open their mind to the degree where they can understand your point of view? Have you ever tried to explain your feelings to someone—tell them how you feel about the way they are treating you or the things they are doing to you, and how you would like them to change, but they just do not possess the mindset to even care? If you have, then you understand one of the most profound realities of life, some people just won't listen.

Why won't some people listen to you? Why do they not care about what you have to say? Why won't they care about what you are about? Why do they not care about the fact that what they are doing to you is hurtful or painful or debilitating to your life? The obvious answer is selfishness. But, I believe it goes much deeper than this, it illustrates who they truly are.

Here is a fact about some/many people, they only care about themselves. Even if they pretend to care about someone else, they are doing this because they are getting something that they want from that individual. Thus, though they may appear to be loving and caring to a specific person, what they are actually doing is simply doing what they do to get what they want.

How about you? How do you behave towards other people? How do you treat them? How do you listen to them? Do you actually care about what they feeling, equaling what they are saying? And, moreover, what's in it for you? What do you get out of the way you behave towards them?

Many people never contemplate any of this. They do what they do, thinking of nothing but what they are thinking about. Through time, you can really see this in the overall presentation of a person's life; defined by what they have done. What have they done? Is what they have done based upon goodness and helpful loving kindness. Or, is what they have done based upon all of the other bad things of life: selfishness, hurtful behavior, vanity, judgment, and crime?

The answer to who and what a person is becomes very obvious by viewing what they do.

This leads us to the next level of understanding personal behavior. How do you feel about what that other person has done? Do you revel in their attacks on others? Do you cheer them on when they do some self-serving, selfish action? Do you applaud them when they hurt someone else?

Here's a fact, just because you do not like someone, does not mean you have the right to hurt them, as hurt only equals and creates more hurt. If you (or anyone) hurts, that means you are not listening to that other individual.

This brings us back to the central point of all this, why do some people not listen?

Have you ever tried to explain something that matters to you and that other somebody dismissed your understandings? Have you ever gotten angry, maybe yelled and scream at someone simply because you wanted them to understand what they were doing to you was damaging but even with this they did not change?

Each person is based in who they are. In many cases, people pretend to be something they are not. This is especially the case at the outset of a relationship. That individual wants something from that other person. Whether it is friendships, love, sex, a job, money, to be in their presence simply because they are in the inner circle, or whatever... But, whatever it is, they want that something from that someone else so they play the game to be the person that other person would want to associate with. Then, through time and relationship evolution the true darkness in that person comes out. Who they truly are is presented. This may occur in an hour, a day, a week, or years into the relationship, but who they are becomes witnessed and known. Then what? If this person does not care about what the other person (what you) are feeling; what can you do?

The answer is really simply, there is nothing that you can do to change them. Who they are is who they are. What they are is what they are. If they cannot bring themselves to care about what another individual (what you) are feeling, this will not change.

Is this a personality defect? Of course it is. Is this the way people should behave? Of course not. But, if Not Caring is a definition of their personality, if the ability to not feel for the other person is what defines their mind, this will never change.

So, what are we (what are you) left with? We can leave the relationship if we can. Though this may be the best answer, this is not always possible. Then what? The only answer is for you to be the bigger person—for you to care about them even though they do not and cannot truly care about you. Listen to them, even though they will not listen to you. Because no matter how much you talk, yell, scream, smash your fist into the wall, nothing will change if a person does not care enough to care about you.

In closing, when people speak, listen. Listen to what they are saying and truly try to understand their point of view. As long as what they saying is not based in selfishness, ego, or hurtful thoughts and actions, don't you think they should, at least, be listened to? If they are speaking about the way you are treating them, and what you are doing is hurtful or debilitating or not helpful, again listen. Remove your ego, care about them. Stop thinking only about yourself and what you are feeling and experience. Hear what they have to say.

The Things You Wish You Never Saw
14/Nov/2022 07:55 AM

I don't know about you, but I like to see happy things—things that make me smile and feel good. Whether that is a photograph, a movie, some positive words written on a page, somebody loving their dog or their cat, or just a passing visual or audio something that takes place in my field of reality.

I don't know about you, but I don't like to see negative things—things that make me cringe inside. Whether that is a hurtful photograph, a horror, thriller, or drama movie where people are hurt or killed, people doing bad things to other people out on the street, or just negative words that are written.

For me, whenever I encounter the positive stuff, I really like to soak it in—allow it to make me smile for a while. The negative stuff, I just switch the channel. I don't want to see it, experience it, or read it.

I don't know about you, but every now and then I'll be scanning my social media whatever and I will see someone that is in my, *"Friends,"* or, *"Followers,"* or my, *"Whatever,"* really showing or saying something negative about someone or something. This always really surprises me because I always try to surround myself with positive people. Sure, we all have our moments, but if you are walking the path of positivity, if you are living your life consciously, you don't allow that kind of stuff to take hold of you to the degree where you either produce or disseminate that level of negativity out to the outside world.

Generally, when this kind of thing occurs, I just cut them out of my realm of reality, so I am never impact with that level of STUFF, at least not from that person, ever again. Sometimes, however, for whatever reason, I've got to keep them in my spear of reality. So, I don't, *"Unfollow."* But, once that person has unleashed something like that, I am always very weary of them. Why would they believe that their thoughts, their feelings, their opinions, their art, their whatever, based in negativity, should be unleashed to the world? Doesn't that show that they are not living their life from the perspective of Goodness?

We all have a choice that we can choose. Your life is your life and what you do with it is what you choose to do with it. As you have a choice, isn't it better to make the choice to only spread the positive, the good, the beautiful, and the happy-making? Sure, you may have your opinions, you may like or dislike what you like or dislike, but it's you who spreads what you spread out to the world. From this, an entirely new reality of feelings is unleashed and given birth to in other people.

Who do you want to be? The person who makes other people feel good? Or, the person who churns up negativity in the hearts, the emotions, and the feelings of others? If you are a person of consciousness, if you are a person who cares, I believe the answer to that question is obvious.

Be Positive! Only spread positivity!

* * *

13/Nov/2022 07:08 AM

If you're expecting a person to be the perfect expression of what you expect them to be, you will always be disappointed.

*   *   *
13/Nov/2022 07:07 AM

If you can't forgive a person for who they are, you should never allow them to be a part of your life.

Casting the Script of Life
10/Nov/2022 08:18 AM

I came upon this article I wrote sometime back that you may find interesting.

For anyone who has ever thrown their hat into the Hollywood ring of acting they can quickly detail that when someone is casting for a film, they provide a fairly detailed view of what they are looking for. For anyone who has ever been on the other side of the camera, creating a movie, they know that when they are casting a character in a film, they have an image in their mind of how that character will look and how that character will behave. Look on any of the Breakdown Services that come out from the industry and each character has a name and a description. Filmmakers are looking for what they want that character to look like and actors are trying to become that character.

In traditional industry casting session, you will find an untold number of similar looking people vying for the same role. Casting offices are full of them. And, this goes on everyday.

To be cast in a film the generally process is a hopeful actor is given what are known as, *"Sides."* This is a limited amount of dialogue taken from the script. The actor then practices those lines, gets into a self-created costume, shows up at the casting office, waits with all of the other actors that look and sound just like them, and finally goes in to, *"Read."*

That's the game. People try to become the character in hopes of getting the role. But, most people do not get the role. In fact, some people go to an untold number of auditions and never get a role. They do this, spending all that time and all that money, until they finally give up. What did it all prove?

In some cases, once an actor has developed a name for himself or herself, they are allow to play a role completely off-script. Think about it; think about some of the films you have seen where one of the known Name actors has not looked at all right for the role. Maybe it was their hair. Maybe it was their beard. Maybe it was their size. But, because of the fact that they had a, *"Name,"* they were asked to portray the role simply to bring buzz to the film. And, that's all part of the game. The game of casting for life. People try to become while some people have already become. Some people will never become while others have become and do not even realize or care about what they have become.

Think about your life. Think about who you are attempting to become. Think about what you are attempting to portray. Is what you are projecting to the world actually you or is it simply and image of a person created by someone else—a person you are pretending to be?

In life, we all do all kinds of things to be seen the way we wish to be seen. This is what leads to lies, this is what leads to overspreading on clothing, this is what leads to anorexia, this is what leads to bad haircuts.

The thing that most people never take the time to realize—never have the capacity to realize is that what anyone projects is not necessarily a true representation of themselves. It is simply a game they are playing that is then projected to the world. How about you? What do you do to solidify your projection to the world? How does that projection contrast to who you really are? And, who really knows the truth about who you really are? Do you?

We are each two things. We are who and what we are in our minds. And, we are who and what we are that we project to the world. Some people are very true to themselves. But, these people are very few. Most simply lie about the truth that they project. They lie to themselves and they lie to others.

So, here's the test. Who are you? Who are you really? What are you? What are you really? Who and what do you project to the world? Who knows who and what you truly are? Are you simply an actor attempting to get cast in a film and pretending to be something you are not or are you truly you? If you do not have a clear and honest definition of this you do not have a clear definition of your life.

Tomato Soup on the Road to Never Stop Learning
10/Nov/2022 07:05 AM

Probably like most of you, I've been eating tomato soup my whole life. When I was a little kid, I began to cook it for myself out of a *Campbell's* can. As the years went on, and canned soup got better, I moved over to *Progresso* and brands like that, then to the fresh soups offered in the Dairy/Deli section of the supermarkets. Though I've never been a super big fan of tomato soup, sometimes in restaurants, and places like that, I have had some pretty tasty tomato soup.

As I'm pretty much the chef around my home… …It's kind of funny, every now and then, when my lady and I are in supermarkets and places like that, and the cashier (or someone) will make some comment about what is she planning to cook? I have to immediately chime in, *"She never cooks anything!"* Some people just are not about cooking. That's fine. I don't mind.

Anyway, throughout the many years of my life, whenever I have made tomato soup as a side dish or something, I've kept it fairly basic. …Boring and basic. A lot of times I just hand a good portion of it over to my lady, *"You want this?"*

Recently, I don't know what it is, but I began to explore some tomato soup recipes. I discovered that it is really easy to make some very tasty tomato soup. Which is something I've now been doing over the last little while. I even had some for lunch today. I mean, with just a few additional ingredients, you can really turn the favor around. …Making it really-really good.

What I'm saying here is, most of us just do things the way we do things all of our life. We find a pattern and that is what we do. Whether it's good, bad, or otherwise doesn't really matter. We do what we do until we can do it no longer. That's really sad, I think. Just like my life with tomato soup,

I have missed out on so much flavor. …Missed out, because I did not explore the new ways to DO.

So… Here's my suggestion… Today, find out how to do something differently. Shake up your life of doing everything the same. It can be something as simple as how you make tomato soup, or it can go up the ladder from there.

Catch yourself today, doing what you do the same way all the time, and then STOP. Check out if there is a way to do it differently.

You never know, like me with tomato soup, you may discover a new and better path, that is very easy to follow, leading to a much more flavorful life.

When You Lose Your Favorite Toy
09/Nov/2022 07:14 AM

Ever since I've settled into a more sedentary life and lifestyle, I've always had at least two cats. Sometimes, as the years tick on, they pass away and move onto the other/outer realms that no one really knows anything about. But, they are gone... When this happens, after the grief has somewhat subsided, though it may take some time to find the right partner, we always get a new friend for our remaining cat. No matter what anyone says, cats are not solitary creatures. They need a friend.

Each cat that has been in my life has its own very unique personality. Just like people, each cat is their own person—they like what they like, and they dislike what they dislike.

We have this cat that came into our life about a year ago. A sweet little girl with just an adorable personality—one of those beings that you just can't help but love. She's a player. She likes to play with us. She likes to play with her roommate. They chase each other back and forth. And, she likes to play by herself.

Since she has joined us, it was necessary to assemble this big pile of cat toys: balls, strings, little stuffed animals, and various other stuff. The toys are all situated over in one corner that I call her toy box. I always exclaim to her that she needs to put her toys away when she's done playing with them because all it takes is like an hour or two and they're all over the place. Of course, she doesn't listen to me. It's always me that must pick them up and put them away.

I was sitting on the couch today, eating lunch, and out of the corner of my eye I see her playing with her favorite stuffed ball toy. It has a little string attached to it and she runs around, bapping it all over the place. I see her run it out to the patio. She's up on her hind legs slapping it around. Then, she swipes it hard and she knocks it over the side of the patio. I shake my head, put down my quesadilla, and get up.

Where I live there is this massive forest of vines and plants and stuff down below my patio. I look down but I could not see it. Meaning, if I can't see it from up here there is no way I could find it down there. It's gone. Her favorite toy has been sent to never-never-land. Sad…

Now, I don't know how she feels about losing her favorite toy. She did sit there for a time looking over the side where she had knocked it away. But me, I feel bad. I mean it's so hard to lose your favorite toy. I know I have had my toys taken away in the past and it doesn't feel good.

I remember the first time that this happened, I was like three or something and father got mad at me, for some reason, (I mean really, what can a three-year-old that is all that bad?), but he grabbed my hobby horse from me broke it over his knee. I was crushed. I really loved that hobby horse. When I was like ten, my mother got mad at me, again for who knows what reason, and she picked up and smashed my favorite model car that I had built. I was so sad, I had put so much work into that model and really like looking at it. When I was maybe eleven or twelve my bike got stolen. I really loved that bike. It was a *Schwinn Pea Picker*. When I was in my twenties my girlfriend caught me cheating on her (again). I was a horrible womanizer back then. She crashed her way through the front door of my apartment and grabbed the first thing she could find, which was my favorite guitar, and she smashed it into a thousand pieces. Very sad. I loved that guitar. Of course, there's been people who ran into my motorcycles and my cars that I really loved; destroying them. But, whatever the cause, don't you think it is really sad when you lose your favorite toy—even if, like my cat just did, you do it to yourself? How about you? What, *"Toy,"* have you lost that you really loved?

There is all this anti-material spiritualism out there that you can reference about how you should not become attached to physical objects. Or, like Bob Dylan sang, *"When you ain't got nothing, you got nothing to lose."* But, who can feel that way all time? When something is lost that you love, it is gone forever. And though, maybe you try to replace it, (I know I have), any replacement is just that, a replacement. It's not that true love.

So, I don't know??? We are all going to lose things those things that we love somewhere along the way. And though, through time, we may be able to rationalize our way out of feeling really-really bad about that loss. But, the loss is still there and it is us (you and I) who must come to terms with that loss.

I guess the main thing is, never be the person who causes anyone to lose that thing that they love. Never be the thief. Never be the destroyer. Never be the hurter. Sure, give people things that they may come to love. But, never be the remover of that love. And, if you can, try to replace that lost, loved toy for that somebody else. Because I think we all are the same, we feel bad when we lose our favorite toy.

* * *
09/Nov/2022 06:50 AM

Do you pet your cat or dog because you want to make them feel happy or do you do it because you want to make you feel happy?

Let Me Criticize You
08/Nov/2022 06:44 AM

From my observation, there are basically two types of people who pass through life: those who appreciate and those who criticize. Sure, sure, a lot of people fall somewhere in-between. But, the essence of the dynamic basically breaks down to those two factors. The Yin and the Yang if you will.

As an artist, my work has found its lovers and its critics. That's just the way it is, and it doesn't bother me that much. For example, from a filmmaking perspective, like virtually all filmmakers will question of their critics, "How many movies have you made?" I mean, because if you actually had made a movie I am sure I could find something wrong with it. As an author, I would ask, *"How many books do you have in the Library of Congress?"* And, you can take this basis of questions to any level of the arts. There are those who do and then there are those who view. And, of course, the doers are also undoubtedly the viewers.

Where do you find yourself in the quandary between appreciator and critic? And, how do you allow that to define your life?

This is where these delineations really come into play. How does what you do and how you view the world define your existence? How does it cause you to act and to react?

From my experience, those who find themselves on the appreciator side of the equations are those who look and learn from all they encounter. They grow from each life experience: from all the see, all they meet, and all they do. The critics, however, only look to find fault. Thus, this comes to be the definitive factor of the life of a person who follows that path.

We all like what we like and dislike what we dislike. Whether it is movies or books or paintings or whatever, we are drawn to a specific expression of that art form. You can find fault in even the most expensive and elaborate of films, if you look for it. Certainly, this is the case with paintings and other visual art forms. You may like the way words are written on a page of a book or you may not. Some songs you like, some you don't. The only problem that arises in this mindset of like and dislike comes about when it keeps you from appreciating the artist's/the creator's own truth. This occurs when you believe you should hold the voice of that creator and dictate as to whether what they have created is good or bad.

From the perspective of an artist, we each try to bring what is in our mind onto the canvas of life; by whatever art form we embrace. Of course, we are defined by all of the things that all lives are outlined by: availability, money, what we have to work with, and so on. But, the individual who bears the need to creates is actually creating something. Those who do not, do not. Yet, some of those who do not create find their voice in criticism. …Which is fine, that's life. But, if that criticism is keeping a person from learning, from growing, from evolving, from experiencing a new way to look at things, then what is left? Stagnation.

What I am saying here is, do not let the critic in you keep you from opening your mind and embracing art at its truest level? If you allow all art, all composed words, all expansive visual whatever simply to be what it is, with no judgement, then by allowing it to be what it is, you enter into a space of elevated consciousness whereby you can appreciate any art for what it truly embodies; art. By removing your judgmental mind, and you trying to decide what that artist should or should not have done, you allow not only yourself, but the artist, and all of the world, to exist on a much higher level of mindfulness, whereby all things are simply allowed to be what they are.

*   *   *

08/Nov/2022 06:44 AM

Everything begins by trying.

Embracing the Positive
07/Nov/2022 06:46 AM

    Here in the United States, the midterm election are taking place tomorrow. Because of this, and due to this fact, the airwaves have been bombarded with commercials about one politician attacking another politician and one cause lambasting the political measure on the opposite side. Everyone I know is just so sick of it. They're all saying, *"I can't wait for Wednesday,"* the day after the election as then the commercials will probably be gone. Though, as we undoubtedly all understand, there is a lot of turmoil in politics across the globe at this point in history. Though the election may be over on Wednesday, there will, more than likely, just be some new form of conflict to infest and attack our minds.

    All this is very emblematic of what is taking place in society. Forget the midterms, look around you, look at how many people are judging, condemning, and saying negativing things about some other person or subject. How about you? How much negativity do you propagate? Who have you hurt, who have you tried to hurt, because that is what words, based in negativity, are meant to do? Is that the right thing to have done?

    Everybody believes their point of view is the right point of view. Okay… So what! Yeah, you believe what you believe. You are programmed to believe that what you believe is right. Yeah, there may be one, two, or a million other people believing as you believe, there may even be commercials on the TV and the radio broadcasting that what you believe is right, but who really cares? At the root of all of life is simply you existing in a space where you are safe, feed, warm in the winter, cool in the summer, and maybe even happy. But, all of that has nothing to do with what anybody says about anyone else, especially if what they are saying is hurtful and negative. That is just Mind Junk that some people get addicted to spewing simply because they can.

Take a moment right and think about the words you are hearing and reading in the outside, out around you. Think about what you heard today, yesterday, last week, last year. How much of what you are listening to or reading is based in negativity? Even more important, how much has what you have heard and what you have read affected what you think and what you have said? If you are believing the beliefs of someone else, if you are following the beliefs of someone else, especially if they are based in negativity, doesn't that mean that you have relinquished the right to be your own person and create your own life based upon your own set of life experiences?

Some people thrive on negativity. It is a very powerful tool and a very addictive mindset as by saying something negativity about someone or something else, this allows a person to feel a sense of empowerment and control as they are the one judging and depreciating that other individual or subject. How about you? How do you feel when you criticize or condemn someone else?

Okay, this's what's going on. But, it doesn't have to be that way! Life, your life, the life of those you know and associate with, does not have to be based on negativity! We all understand that living a life based upon negativity never ends well. It always leads one to dark places. Let's change all that!

Take today, forget all the stuff that's going on out there on the airways in politics and otherwise, and let's just be positive! Instead of criticizing anyone, turn that around, say something positive. Even if you don't like a person, say something positive about them. Spread that positivity out to the world. Take today and do not allow yourself to be defined by negativity. Don't say anything negative about anyone or anything. Instead, intentionally say something positive. Even if you have to force yourself to do so, get out there and say or write something positive!

Your life becomes defined by what you do over and over and over again. You can allow yourself to be defined by negativity. Or, you can follow the road that we all understand is better. Be a force of positivity. Today, speak only the positive. You never know, you may like it, and positivity may become the definition of your life.

* * *
05/Nov/2022 07:27 AM

What do you dream about when you're sleeping in heaven?

* * *
04/Nov/2022 05:57 PM

If you are saying anything negative about anybody for any reason you are NOT making anything any better.

Only Fond Memories
02/Nov/2022 02:35 PM

  I just found out that one of my closest friends passed away this morning. We had been friends for over fifty years. It is really one of those strange emotions that comes over someone (me), it's like what do you do with these feelings?
  My friend had been on the wrong side of health for a lot of years. He started smoking when he was like twelve or thirteen. And, he smoked up into his fifties when he had to get his first heart stint. He drank a lot of hard alcohol throughout his life. Hell, when we were still in Hollywood High School, we would arrive at our friend's house every Friday night and pound beer after beer all weekend, showing up to class on Monday morning more than disheveled. Not, to mention all the stories I can tell of wild weekends we lived at the birth of the Punk era in Hollywood and the long lost weekends (weeks) in San Francisco, Vegas, Vancouver, and Victoria. We partied! But, we lived two very different lives. He never worked out like I did. He never strived to eat heathy foods. He never shunned the bad stuff that many ingest.
  He had a couple of heart stints. His kidneys were gone. He had lost part of one of his feet to diabetes, and I guess it all finally caught up with him. But, no matter how clear all the oncoming signs of demise are, you never think that your friend is actually going to die. Especially when it happens in a flash. He was in the hospitable having one of his stints replaced and I am told, after the operation was completed, he was in recovery and he went into cardiac arrest. He was revived once but then it happened again and that time they could not save him.
  When I was three, and in the hospitable after surgery for a broken elbow, I am told I went into cardiac arrest. I guess I woke up, didn't know where I was or something, freaked out, and my heart turned off. But, I lived. I have always wonder why?

My father died instantly from a heart attack. He was at work, and he just keeled over. His work-friend came knocking at our door in tears, telling us he was gone.

Death is never easy. At least not easy for those of us who are still alive.

After his brother called me, telling me the news, all I could think about was that all I have is fond memories of the guy. I knew him forever and even though we didn't hang out all that much in these later years, I always knew he was there, and he knew I was here.

I think that is probably the main thing you have to focus on in life, developing fond memories. That's why you never want to hurt anyone. Be kind. I mean, you really need to be good to all people. You really need to smile. You really need to be there for them and to help them and to care about them. Because at the end of the day, we are all going to check out from this place we call life. How we are remembered is all that we will leave behind.

Things You Used to Own
02/Nov/2022 08:37 AM

Have you ever had one of those thoughts come to your mind where you remember something that you used to own and you wish that it was still in your possession? I think we probably all have encounter that feeling at some point. ...Unless, of course, you are some sort of a massive hoarder and you have never let go of anything. From this feeling, a couple of questions arise: why did you let it go in the first place and should you try to buy another?

The pursuit of possessions has always been looked down upon in virtually all spiritual traditions. So, if you are like me, having spent your life in those circles, you are constantly reminded that materialism is a bad thing. This being said, it becomes a very fine line between things that you want and things that you need. Then, and because of this, the question must be asked, should you try to replace that item?

For some, replacement is easy. Maybe that once owned item was a toy you really loved and you can find another one on some online buying website. Sure, maybe it will cost a few dollars, but it is not some untouchable fee. So, you can buy it. But, then what?

For others, like me, the things I once had and own no more, are items like vintage guitars, which have gone through the roof in price. Something I sold for a thousand dollars twenty-five years ago is now twenty, thirty, or even more times that original number, putting it out of my financial reach. It's the same with some of the cars I owned, that I really loved, without a whole lot of disposable income I can never even come close to replacing that vehicle. Then what? What if you can't afford to get it back?

Life is a constant pathway of doing things and having things done to you. It is what is left after the fact that comes to define the rest of your life. The truth is, we must all deal with the what comes next. ...The what comes next after whatever it is that was done. What do you do?

Take a moment right now and think about that something you had, but you have no more, and you wish you owned again. If you do not possess this feeling, count yourself very lucky. If you can turn this feeling off, rationalize it out of your mind, good for you! But, if you can't, think about it. What did you have that you wish you had again?

Once that thought is in your mind, break it down: why did you have to let it go? Was it stolen from you? Did it fall and break? Did you give it away? Did you sell it? If it was you who let it go, why did you let it go?

For many, possessions are stolen from our lives in the many ways that can occur. Sometimes, somebody wants something we own and because we care about that person, we give it away. In other cases, we need money or we need more space, so we sell it. Whatever the causation, why were you willing to let that item go, back then, and now why do you wish you had not? Really chart this out.

Now, take this to the next level... You had something that you have no more. What would happen, what would your life be like, if you had it again? Really think this through... Why do you want it back? What would it mean to you? What would it mean to your future? And, what would it cost you and your life to get it back? What will be different in your life if you did have it again? And, is it worth the price you will have to pay?

Most people just DO in their life. They rarely truly think things through. The problem with living your life, defined by this mindset is, however, then, often times, what is done is desired to be undone. How about you? How about that thing(s) you once had and wish to possess again? What unthinking, unthought-out desire was in play that caused you to lose that item in the first place?

Okay... Now, what are you going to do with all of this? You had it. You want it back. Now what?

Here we reach the critical part of this dilemma. As discussed, most people just DO without thinking. Is that what you are doing right now in association with that re-wished for item? Or, is this a conscious decision made in an effort to regain that something lost in your life that will not only make your today a better place but also your tomorrow?

Many people, in their Life Time, play the same melodrama over and over and over again. They refuse to allow themselves to evolve. By looking to your past, is that what you are doing? By regaining what you had in your past, will that cause you to make the same mistakes that caused you to lose that re-desired item in the first place?

For each person, the answer to these questions is different. For each person, the life-response to their desires is different. But, if you do not very consciously chart out what you are doing as you desire to regain what was lost in your past, you may very well find yourself stuck in the same situation that created you to loss that something in the first place. Think about it.

Imitation is not Flattery it's Just Appropriation
01/Nov/2022 02:17 PM

I was flipping channels the other night and I watched a few minutes of the great Oliver Stone film, *The Doors*. I came in around the time when Kyle MacLachlan's character, who was portraying Ray Manzarek, made mention of Jean-Luc Godard. (I actually saw the movie for the first time in the theatre with Ray Manzarek. But, I've spoken about that in other places). Anyway… Amazingly, Godard just died a little over a month ago. He was certainly one of the greatest figures in causing modern cinema to evolve. You can read all about his history, the French New Wave, the Dziga Vertov Group, and all that on-line, so I won't go into any of that here. But, if you are a student of film or a lover of cinema, you really need to check him and his work out.

The thing about Godard, and other filmmakers who worked to push the craft of filmmaking to new levels of exploration, is that they had their critics. I mean, Godard was very outspoken about his political and philosophic beliefs. His group even got the Cann Film Festival to shut down for a moment in 1968. This being said, he came up in a time when experimentation was applauded and appreciated. From this, he could lean into his artistic tendances and forge new realms in cinema that may not have been explored had he attempt to create in another time and a different geographic environment.

I know I have been asked many times, (and I am not comparing myself to Godard on any level), if I thought that had I been based in Europe would my cinematic creative vision of *Zen Filmmaking* have found a more appreciative audience? I always dismiss that question, as I know my reality is simply my reality. Like Popeye said, *"I yam what I yam,"* and I lived in the time and the place where I existed. Sure, it would have been nice to have found myself in a time of a global mindset where the exploration of new forms of art was more embraced. But, that was not the case. And certainly, there have been those that have understood and liked what I was doing and what I am doing. And, I thank them! But, it seems we are living in a period of time where people find more truth in criticism than in the creation of art.

One of the things that I find interesting in all of this, and the reason I write this piece, is that there have been a number of people who have criticized my work and myself, yet they go out there and attempt to mimic by Zen creative vision. They do this while giving me no credit. Interesting...

As I have long said, *"Criticism is easy. Making a movie is hard work."* And, *"What is a film critic? With very few exceptions it is someone who doesn't have the talent or the dedication to actually make a movie."* Yet, a few have. They attempt to imitate my process, while providing no reference to their source of inspiration. They do this while criticizing my work. Okay???

It's kind of like in the world of martial arts, where criticism reigns supreme. I have certainly had my detractors. But, all of my detractors have never practiced anything I teach; in my books or via other methods. They may have read my articles or my books, but they have not tried to actually put the techniques I illustrate into practice. Again, criticism is easy. Doing is much harder. The ones who have attempted to put the techniques into practice, have learned new things. And, that's what life is all about; isn't it?

Talk is cheap and that's why so many make a name for themselves by doing it. But, what are they truly giving to the world? A new form of art? No. A new evolution or interpretation of artistic understanding? No. Just talk.

Speaking of the martial arts, I think back to this one so-called teacher a number of years ago. When my book *Samurai Zen* came out, he was apparently teaching some of the methods presented in that book. When some of his students inquired where he received the knowledge, did he get it from my book? He told them that, *"No, I was his student."* Funny… I had never met then man. …Had never even heard of him. I also later found out that he was criticizing the book and me. This, while he was teaching techniques he had learned from it.

You know, we all learn from someone. Once we learn we then take that knowledge and hopefully not only put it to use but then expand upon it and develop our own personal realizations that we may then spread out to the world based upon the initially knowledge that was provided to us. But, if you can't honor the source of your knowledge, what does that say about you? If you do not give credit where credit is due, imitation is not a form of flattery, it is simply an appropriation.

How Quickly Can You Find Your Meditative Mind?
01/Nov/2022 09:39 AM

In each of our lives we encounter situations that cause us to lose our peace. Yes, you can train your mind to not become upset. But, most people don't.

Here's the thing, ask yourself, why do you become upset? The answer, you do not like what is taking place. Whether this is brought about what is happening to your life via some abstract something or it comes at you from someone doing something that you do not like, most people lose their peace from time to time. That's just the reality of life.

The simple remedy for this is, refuse to care. Think about it... Think about something that you became upset about... If you didn't care, you wouldn't care. Right?

The thing about this mindset is, however, it is a Mind Game. It is you causing you to remove yourself from the most animalistic nature of your being and rising to the level of control where you elevate yourself to the position of administrator of what you feel. Meaning, you stop the feelings that you do not want to feel.

Though this is a powerful tool, most people never choose to develop the ability to actualize it. Thus, they allow themselves to be controlled by the Out There instead of the In Here.

Another pathway towards control of the mind and its emotions is that of, Removal. This is why people move to monasteries, ashram, and the like. Removed from the things that the average person is forced to encounter on a daily basis, they are allowed to move deeper into the more spiritual realms of reality as they are not confronted with the sporadic randomness defined by the majority of those who inhabit the regions of the common world where a person's only concern is themselves and from this selfish and bad doings are enacted.

Most people do not possess the inclination to live a life that removed from the states of common and accepted reality, however. Thus, most are left dealing with the realities and the conflicts found in day-to-day life.

If this is your case, then what are you left with? How can you live in the world but not be dominated by the world?

Ask yourself, how quickly can you find your meditative mind? Have you ever even embraced your meditative mind? Do you commonly step into your meditative mind? Truly, what is your answer to these questions? Because your answer to these questions will detail the level of reality you are currently living.

In truth, most people never attempt to find the space of peace present within their meditative mind. Most do not meditate. There are a million reasons for this, but that does not change the fact. The problem arises, if you do not meditate, then you have chosen to develop no control over your mind. From this, you are defined by the whims of your mind. You are defined by the emotions present in your mind; evoked by whatever external stimuli you may encountered: good or bad. If you have not developed the ability to consciously step into your meditative mind at will, that, in and of itself, provides you with the definition of your life and why you will constantly be swayed by what is taking place outside of yourself.

Each of us, in our lives, will experience things that we do not like. That is human nature. But, it is what we do with those experiences, internally, that will set the definition of our life and will dictate what will happen next in our life.

Do you meditate? If you do not, why don't you? Seriously, why do you not meditate? If you do meditate, how long does it take you to find your mediative mind?

The fact of the fact is, the more you meditate, the quicker you will be able to embrace that spiritual place of human existence where you are not dominated by the external goings on of the world around you.

Which do you believe is better, being force into feelings and then being wholly controlled by those feelings, instigated by whatever external experience you may find yourself encountering? Or, no matter how frustrating you may find a particular life experience to be, possessing the ability to control yourself to the degree where you can guide yourself into the mindset where peace and silence may be experienced instead of turmoil and desperation?

Meditation is not hard. In fact, it is perhaps one of the easiest things to do in life. Yet, so few people learn how to do it. Through practice and developed technique if you can train yourself to quickly and readily enter your meditative mind you will be able to shield your life from random attacks of self-propelled emotional sabotage and come to a state of tranquil understanding.

Meditate, you may be able to find a new world where you are no longer dominated by the whims, desires, bad doings, and bad attitudes of others. Meditate and you may be able to experience the profound wisdom of silence.

* * *
31/Oct/2022 09:20 AM

What if you were to get a ticket, (like a speeding ticket), every time you did something wrong, hurt someone, lied, or did something negative? How many tickets would you have collected throughout your life?

*   *   *

31/Oct/2022 07:35 AM

Do you surround yourself with things you need, or do you surround yourself with things you want?

You Can't Teach Here
30/Oct/2022 08:24 AM

Back when I was with the Integral Yoga Institute, we, of course, all practiced hatha yoga and meditation together on a regular basis. Most of us, myself included, when we first got involved with Swami Satchidananda and his teachings, we did so by taking some of the various classes on yoga taught at the Institute. As is always the case in life, some people simply possess the nature to spread what they have learned outwards to others. And, they may do that without having received any formal certificate or permission to do so.

There was this one very nice lady and her husband who became involved with the Institute. They came around frequently and eventually got to meet Gurudev and stuff like that. Hatha Yoga Teacher Training came around. But, as it turns out, this lady had already been teaching yoga to a group of people. Yoga techniques that she had learned from the IYI. She had been doing this before ever receiving teacher training. Did this mean that what she was doing was wrong? Did this mean that what she was doing was somehow lacking? Or, did this mean that she was simply mimicking the training she had received, in the classes she had taken, and was spreading this knowledge out to the world?

As the teacher training course was just beginning, she mentioned this fact to the instructor—the fact that she had been teaching. Her question was raised, now what? It nicely went around a little bit, but it came down to the fact that once she had completed the teaching training she would have to start giving the IYI a good portion of the money she was charging for teaching those classes. The lady eventually fell away and did not complete the course. Did that make her ability to teach hatha yoga any less?

In the martial arts, it is quite common that a student will earn a black belt and immediately break away from their instructor to open their own school. In some systems, the student is encouraged to do this to spread the brand and to funnel money-earned back to the headmaster. In other cases, however, this is not the case. The student just breaks away and opens their own school in order to focus on themselves, and in some instances, to denigrate or depreciate their previous instructor. They do this long before they have spent the years in training to earn the fourth-degree black belt which is understood to be the point where an advanced student becomes an instructor. Is what they are doing wrong?

If you look to the realm of spirituality, there have been many noted western teachers who traveled to the East and/or learned what they learned from various eastern-based teachers. Some formed a conglomeration of what they learned and spread it to others. There are those who have criticized these teachers as not having learned the full-system of understanding before they began broadcasting it to the world. Even respected orators like Gurdjieff had their critics—those who claimed that he was teaching an incomplete system because he had not yet mastered the teaching he was disseminating. True or not, he had an untold number of followers who, to this day, study his teachings. And, that is just one example. Was what he was doing wrong?

Some people simply possess the nature to be a teacher. Some people do this based in ego, while others do this based in a true dedication to a subject. If you look to the dissemination of yoga in the western world, for example, many teachers were (and are) not formally qualified to teach. If you look at the primary propagation of the martial arts in the western world, some of the early, formative personas, did not even possess their black belt when they began to teach. Was that wrong?

The first question you must ask yourself when you find yourself studying from someone is, are you learning something of value to you? Then you must question, is the person who is teaching you worthy of the title of teacher? But then, the deeper question arises, if you are learning from someone who is not wholly qualified to teach, what are you not learning?

For those of us who walk the life path of knowledge, we want to know—we are constantly studying and attempting to get to the source of knowledge where our own realizations may be born. Can we learn from anyone? Or course. You can always learn from anyone you encounter simply by studying what they say, what they do, how they do it, and the impact of what they are saying and doing is having on others. But, does that mean that they are a True Teacher? No, not necessarily. Yes, they may proclaim themselves to be a teacher. But, self-proclamation does not a teacher make.

What does this tell us? For those of us who want to learn, for those of us who want to know, though we can learn from anyone, who we call our teacher must be defined by a grander set of standards. Do not believe someone to be a true teacher simply because they give themselves the title of a teacher and set up a class. Don't believe someone simply because they are in the position of an instructor. Don't follow a person's teachings simply because they have other people believing them. A true teacher has been schooled at the source. They have the support of those they studied from. They pay homage to those teachers they learned from. They are not someone who simply sets up a class and finds the lost, the bored, and the lonely to listen to them.

Study who your teachers truly are.

* * *
30/Oct/2022 07:06 AM

If you don't desire it, don't do it.

If you do desire it, contemplate the consequences of doing it.

How Bad Do You Feel About the Bad Things That You Do?
28/Oct/2022 09:50 AM

How bad do you feel about the bad things that you do? I was thinking about just posting this question and leaving it as a, that-is-that. But then, I thought, let me dig a little bit deeper into the subject.

It seems that life events always seem to happen in clusters. From this, it causes me to be forced to question certain very-specific levels of reality, for a time, in a continuous fashion. So, here we go again…

How bad do you feel about the bad things that you do?

There are people like me, who feel guilty about everything. I mean, even if I tell a joke that someone takes the wrong way, I feel bad about it. Then, there are people on the opposite end of the spectrum; those who just do not care about anybody but themselves and/or they could care less about any damage they do to someone else's life. Some even revel in this power. I have known a number of people like this as I have passed through my life. Most people are somewhere in between. How about you? How bad do you feel about the bad things that you do?

The ultimate question you have to ask yourself is, why do you behave in the manner that you behave? The problem is, most people just live. They base their entire life upon excuses. They justify their actions towards other in oh so many ways. Whether it is their belief that they need to make money, they are doing it to fight for some person or cause, they did it to me so I can do it to them, that they have earned the right, that they feel they hold the justification to overpower someone else in some way, that they just don't care about that anyone or the anything else, or that they are so lost into the realms of their own delusion that they never think about any of this at all. They just do what they do and all others be damned. Again, who are you? And, how do you behave? How often do you ask yourself this question?

If we look around at the world, we see self-serving, hurtful behavior all the time. I am sure you can think about a time or times that it has happened to you. Because it has happened to you, because it has happened to all of us, wouldn't you think that this would cause people, having felt the pain, to not want to unleash it onto anyone else and, thus, become a person who always desires to never hurt anyone and if they do they try to fix it to the best of their ability? But, it doesn't seem that the world is like that, does it? There is hurt going on all the time. There is self-centered behavior going on all around us. There are people doing what they do, only thinking about themselves, and they are justifying their actions, at least in their own mind, by any number of self-defined levels of lies.

Is there an answer? I believe, the only answer begins with you. You must become the catalyst for change. You have to be the place where change is instigated. Because if you don't do it, who else will?

You can make all of the excuses you want, justifying the actions you take for whatever reason you believe to be true. But, if what you are doing hurts someone, what is the ultimate consequence? Answer: You are part of the problem, not part of the cure.

Most of us do not intentionally go out of our way to do hurtful things. For the ones who do, they should be condemned, not celebrated. But, those people are a very small percentage. This being said, there are times when we all may, unintentionally, do some damage to someone else's life. It is what we do next that defines the ultimate course of those life events. You can try to fix it, or you can lie, deny, and/or just not care. Who are you? How bad do you feel about the bad things that you do?

It is you who sets the standard for how your life, and the lives of all those you encounter, will be lived. You can care enough to care and/or you can forever try to set the standard for making things right. This is not to say that if you are the good person, if you strive to do the right thing, that adversity brought on by someone else may not find you. But, with you attempting to be a beacon of light, what you project to the world, and the people you interact with, will always be remember as good and never hurtful.

How bad do you feel about the bad things that you do? Your life. Your choice.

Sorry Doesn't Mean Much Unless You Make It Mean Something
26/Oct/2022 09:48 AM

A lot of people do a lot of hurtful things in this world. In some cases, they are intentional, in other cases they are not. Some people never own the damage and the hurt they create. Others, understand their wrongness and try fix what they have unleashed. *"I'm sorry,"* is the first step. But, *"Sorry,"* doesn't mean much unless you make it mean something.

You hear it all the time, people saying, *"That person got their karma,"* or, *"They paid their debt to society."* But, as I have long said, what does that mean to the victim? Does a person getting some sort of karmic retribution or a person getting out of jail after doing their time fix any hurt or pain they caused that someone else? No, it does not. So, I say all those kinds of statements are false and meaningless. If an individual does not consciously and directly attempt to fix anything negative they have done, directly to the individual they have done it to, there should not be and cannot be any karmic redemption and/or forgiveness.

I had an interesting (well not really) thing happen to me on Monday. I had hit over to Starbucks to grab a latte, as I usually do each morning. As I was driving out of the parking lot, I hear an interior bang on the front of car. It stops; my car that is. Though the engine was still running, my car would not move. Dead in its tracks. The only problem was, and it was a BIG one, was that my car had died in the middle of the driveway out to the street.

To describe this driveway, it is up, then down out to the street, where the street meets an uphill climb. My car had died right at the top of the incline of the driveway. Thus, I got out and tried to push it, forward or back, but because there were hills on both sides, I was completely stuck. Obviously, I was freaking out. It was a really bad situation as people were coming (or at least trying to) in and out of that parking lot and I was totally blocking the exit lane. But, I could do nothing about it. My car was too heavy for me to push uphill. I was in the middle of a really fucked up situation.

To tell the back story, I had to have the trani on my car redone a couple of months ago. I spoke about in a blog awhile back. I knew they had done a bad job, though I had it done at AAMCO which is one of the biggest trani places here in the States. Here was the proof they had done a bad job. But, this proof had really screwed me over.

I called AAA but they were not going to arrive for over two hours. What! Are you kidding me! I've been paying you money for all of these decades and you promise a thirty minute arrival time but now, for me, it is going to take two hours even though I'm in the middle of this really bad situation! One of the women I spoke to threatened to hang up on me because I was asking why it would take so long in, as she put it, an obviously agitated manner. What! Hang up on me! This is your fault! I am agitated because your people are not going to be here for two hours!

Finally, this big burley guy with long white hair and a long white beard pulls up in his truck and offers to help me. THANKS!!! We rock the car back and forth, to get it off of that hill, and I coasted it back over to the side of the driveway, where at least people could get by me. This is why whenever I see a person broken down by the side of the road or trying to push their car out of the way I always get out to help them, because if you've ever been in that situation, you know how horrible it can be. For me, this was probably the worst car-break-down situation I'd ever been in and I've had my share.

So, with the car, more or less, out of the way, I sat there, steaming in my anger for the next two hours until the tow truck showed up. The guy, who told me he was also a mechanic, lifted my car way up, looked at what was going on, and told me the AAMCO I took my car to had lied and they had not replaced at least one of the axles as they had charged me for and that was the problem, an axle had broken. True or false, I didn't know and didn't really care. I was pissed and though I hoped to never see the people at that AAMCO again, due to the warranty situation, I had to have it towed back to them.

After having encountered a bad experience at that AAMCO, feeling I had really gotten ripped off, I wrote a fairly hardcore, one-star, Yelp review. Though I really hate to write negative reviews, that's the great thing about Yelp, you can get your factual truth out there and maybe save someone else from going through what you had gone through. The manager of the place had called me after he read that review, a couple of months back. I, of course, never picked up. But now, here he was calling me in apology mode, and telling me to get the car to him and he would fix it. He called me twice as I was waiting the two hours for the tow truck.

I went home and later that afternoon I get a call, telling me what the problem was and that it would be fixed ASAP. I thought it was going to take a few weeks like it had the last time I gave them car. So, I went out to get on my motorcycle, to do what I had to do for the day. But, I start to ride off on it and discovered I had a flat. Are you kidding me!

Now, as you may or may not know, a flat on a motorcycle is way more complicated than on a car. You can't just jack a motorcycle up and switch out the tire with the spare, nor can you use that squirt in the tire, fix a flat stuff. You gotta pull the bike apart and get the tire off or pay a few hundred dollars to have it towed to a shop and have it done, which is really the best way to do it as they know how to do it right. So, I was stuck and pissed off. What a day!

By Tuesday, however, the manager at the shop was calling me and telling me he would have the car done that afternoon. *"Wow, thank you!" "All for free, of course,"* he proclaimed and he offered to change the axles and do all the this and that and even give me a free oil change if I wanted one. *"No thanks."* I knew what he was after.

The thing is, he seemed like a nice enough guy. It was just the policies of the business and, I guess, the mechanics he employed, that messed my life up.

So, at 4:30 I go to pick up the car. They did a lot of work in a really short amount of time. It shows you what they can do if they want to. As he walks me out to my car, he speaks about all he has done and how he hopes to keep all his customers happy and the like. Throughout all of our conversation he continues to mention my Yelp review, and I knew the reason he was going full-on to fix, or better put, re-fix my car, was so that I may rewrite that review. I observed, and I knew, it was all a negotiation. As I was about to leave, *"I hope you can do something about the Yelp review,"* he says. *"I'll see what I can do,"* I answer.

After that, some people were telling that I should double down and discuss how not only did they screw me over when fixing my car the first time, and damaging parts on it that I had to have fixed elsewhere, which cost me over a thousand dollars, but that their work is so shabby that my car broke down within two months. There was a part of me that felt I should do that. But, that's just not who I am. In his own way, the manager of the shop was trying to apologize. But, more than that, he was trying to make things right. I appreciated that. Did it undo what I had to go through on Monday? No, not at all. Did it change the fact that they (the shop) cost me a lot of money and did a crappy job? Absolutely not. But, he was trying. And, isn't that all you can ask of a person? Me, I went home and I erased the Yelp review.

So, just keep this in mind as you go through life. *"Sorry,"* means nothing if the person saying it does nothing to repair the damage they created. And, if they (if you) don't say, *"Sorry,"* when you have hurt someone, what does that say about the person you are?

Forgive when forgiveness is warranted. But, never forgive those who hurt you and just do not care.

Teaching What You Know
25/Oct/2022 09:04 AM

Yesterday, I alluded to the fact about shooting a music video on an iPhone and that got me to thinking….

…Thinking about something that I have thought about before. I have long contemplated teaching a course on how to use an iPhone to actually shoot a movie. Though, in truth, I don't know how that would fit into the curriculum of most university programs in cinema, as they like to keep them all-stuffy and stuff. But, as the cameras in iPhones, and smart phones in general, have become so good, in many ways it has become the obvious answer for the low budget filmmaker. …Everyone has one, but few people use them to their full potential.

As time has progressed, there have been filmmakers who have shot movies and music videos on their iPhone and some look really-really good. I'm sure in the plethora of all that, I was one of the first. That statement is not rockin' any ego there or anything. But, as I have always tried to use what was readily available to get a film project completed, the iPhone just became a natural tool. So, when the cameras on the phones got good, I was right there makin' movies with them.

Now that the cameras are really good, and now that pretty much everyone has an iPhone or other high-end smart phone, it has really surprised me that more filmmakers don't use them to get their project completed. If you watch news networks like BBC and the like, you will see that there are reporters out there in the field filming and transmitting their stories via their phone.

I think maybe one of the holdbacks is that people, young or novice filmmakers, want to look professional. So, they want to rock a pro-camera, use a bunch of lights, have a boom operator, and all the stuff like that. And sure, I get it. But, if it is not necessary, it is not necessary. You can make a really good movie, or a whatever, on your phone. You just have to remember to turn it to its side. The major mistake that everyone seems to make is that when they use their phone to film, they hold it in the same vertical position as when they talk to someone or take snapshots. Wrong! That image will not fill a screen. Turn it to its side.

The point in all this being, you can make a really good movie with your phone if you want to. So, for all you filmmakers out there, whether you've made multi-million-dollar movies, no-budge schlock, or just videos of your dog running around, you can do it on your phone, and you can make a quality piece of cinema with it.

Assignment for the day or the whenever... Get out there and film with your phone. Either plan a shoot or when you see a shot, shoot it. Take out your camera, think about shooting it right, and do it! You never know, you may make the next piece of revolutionary cinema. And you may do it with your phone.

Ready for Anything
24/Oct/2022 07:09 AM

A lot of people believe that they can, but they can't. A lot of people believe that they can, but they shouldn't. A lot of people want to do, but very few can actually do. A lot of people live in a space of ego-driven assuredness, but as they do not possess the developed ability to manifest the reality that is held only within their own mind, they can never bring what is in their mind into the realm of physical actuality.

I was watching this reality show, that was shot in Singapore, the year before the pandemic last night. You know, just one those things that don't cause you to think too much; to waste some time before something better comes on the horizon to watch on TV or to do in life.

Anyway, there is this one pop singer on the show who was about to shoot a new music video. She was divided between having this established director or one of her production hopeful friends do the shoot. The pro was ready to go. Her friend, however, as he was inexperienced, was locked in the stage(s) of development. They needed it shot fast, so they went with the pro, through her friend had hyped his hiring, (which he apparently thought he was), up to his family, friends, etc. That's just the backstory for you but has little to do with this piece.

As the girl and her team were discussing the need for the music video to be done quickly, I realized and actually said out loud, *"I could go out there and shoot that music video right now, have it done by morning, and have it edited the next day. Plus, I could shoot it on my iPhone and it would still look great."* Now, this is not about ego, it is about prepared development and the reason why so many people, heading small productions, do not make it through to completion. They don't know what they are doing. They don't know how to make small look big. They do not have the ability to bring what they see in their mind into reality. Or, as in the case with her filmmaking friend, he had some really big ideas, but he did not know how to make them a reality.

Back when I was teaching a lot of courses on filmmaking, I always taught my students that if you cannot go out there and shoot a really good piece with just a camera, and no lights or anything, you do not know how to make a film and you cannot be a true filmmaker. In fact, it was one of the assignments I would give them; to go out and create a Short using nothing but available light. Of course, I would teach them how to work with available light and how to guide it and make it work to their advantage during the course. But, it was them that had to do it. Some of my students created some great projects via that assignment.

Here's the thing, people love to get locked into their mind. They love to write elaborate scripts that could only be filmed with vast budgets. They become lost in the false hope that no-budget will look like big-budget. And sure, there are a lot of people who criticize *Zen Filmmaking*. But, like the friend who hoped to be handed a life-changing music video opportunity, how much cinematic magic have they created? Criticism is easy. Doing is so much harder.

What I am saying here is, in life, at least living the life you hope to live, it is all about developing the ability to DO. It is all about mastering the skills necessary to make what you see in your mind a reality. Then, if an opportunity presents itself, you can say, *"Yes, I can."* And, *"In fact, let's do it right now!"*

Who You Think You Are Compared To Verses Who You Actually Are
23/Oct/2022 06:43 AM

    I was having a latte in the early part of the day, this other day. My lady and I were at this new coffee house that opened up in our area. We were sitting by ourselves on the back outdoor patio of this place when this, (for lack of a better definition), interesting guy walks out and was quite surprised to see that anyone was there. He mumbled something under his breath.
    To describe him, he was one of those people that you could say was dressed to the nines. To the nines, at least by his standards. He was wearing tight black leather pants. A tight black tee shirt. Leopard print shoes with a slight platform. His hair was closely shaved on the sides and the back but tied into a long topknot on the top of his head.
    He was carrying a bounce card, an expensive tripod, and from a well-designed photo backpack he pulled out a high-end DSLR camera. He moved this one table to his desired positioning, opened up his tripod, set up his camera, and put his bounce card into position. Then, he went to order a drink.
    Now, I have no idea what this guy was planning to do. But, it was something. Maybe he was a vlogger, a gamer, who knows??? But, he wasn't working for the business, doing a commercial or anything like that. I guess he just choose this place because it has nicely painted outdoor walls and, as it isn't very popular, he probably thought he would have the whole back patio to himself.
    Not wanting to get in his way. Or, perhaps better put, not wanting to deal with what was to come next, we finished our drinks and left.
    In the parking lot, there was this customized Tesla. It was painted flat black, had custom rims, and the windows

tinted very dark, which is actually illegal here in California. Obviously, that was his car.

So, there he was, a guy totally into himself. Flaunting his stuff. Doing his whatever. Believing he was a, *"Something."* But, was he? Or, was it all something projected from within his own mind?

My question, and the tell-tale sign of the truth of the truth, was, what was missing? Answer: His crew. If he was a true player he would have had his team setting up for him. My guess, he was rolling on daddy's money and possessing a mind locked into a place of self-defined grandeur, where, in there, (and only in there), he was that, *"Something,"* that, *"Character,"* which he was presenting to the world. …An unsuspecting world of people who believe all that they see but do not know the true facts of a guy simply setting up his own equipment, bought with daddy's money, in a restaurant that allows anyone to use their space as long as you buy a coffee.

Think about it? How much do you see? How many people are broadcasting? How many people are pretending they are something, when they are not? How about you?

I think in this day and age it is very easy to pretend. Nobody knows anybody anymore. At least not on an in-person, person-to-person, real level. They just see them on a screen. They see an image that is projected to them and they instantly believe. But, in this immediate belief, there is something missing in creation. The truth of substance has been removed.

But, moreover, and on an even deeper, more important level, what has happened to the truth of humbleness? What has occurred to the individual that only seeks to be a student of the truth, a vessel of wisdom, and not the center of attention? I mean, if you look at life, if you look at all those who scream the loudest about who they believe themselves to be, truly, who are they, what are they? Nothing more than an illusion that they, themselves, have created.

Now, I'm not saying that a person should not work to achieve any goal they may possess. But, where is the truth in self-projection? Where is the wisdom in what they have to say if what they have to say is nothing more than what they think, what they believe, and what they determine the rest of the world should listen to? Isn't that simply a self-determined projection of an ego-driven lie? Remember, a lie, no matter who is telling it, can never become the truth.

So, this is just a passing thought. Something for you to think about as you live your way through your life. Who do you see, telling you what you are listening to, making you believe what it is you believe? Is it a humble person, living a good, selfless, caring, helpful life? Or, is it someone who uses daddy's money to buy a bunch of equipment, (which they have to set up by themselves), drive an expensive car, and project themselves as something more than they actually are?

The truth lies in knowing the truth. How much truth do you know about who you are listening to?

Everybody Has Something to Say but Most People Don't Have Anything Worth Listening To
20/Oct/2022 01:46 PM

I had these two Marshall Amplifiers that I realized I wasn't using. So, I decided to donate them.

Whenever I donate musical equipment, I generally drop it off at this one thrift store over on, what may be defined as, the wrong side of the tracks. I hope to get it into the hands of someone who may not be able to afford that level of equipment. From this, maybe they will be able make some great music with it.

Sure, I know, someone may buy it so they can re-sell it on eBay. But, I try!

Anyway… At this thrift store, they have a cordoned off lane where cars can pull in and someone will help you unload your stuff if you need assistance. Just as I was about to pull into that line, this woman cuts me off and goes into it. Okay… I follow her and watch as she slowly gets out of her car, walks to the passenger side, and begins to look at each piece of clothing she is going to donate. Reading the writing on the wall, I back out, pull up alongside the line, open my truck, grab the amps, load them into the thrift store's containers, and am leaving. The lady exclaims, as I walk by her old PT Cruiser, from the 1990s, that is not in very good condition, *"Blocking traffic so you can do what you want."* Wow, what does that even mean? First of all, I wasn't blocking traffic. There was none. Second of all, there was a major lane for people to pass by me if they wanted to. But, there she was, this aging woman that she felt she had to add some narration to my life. I caught myself staring at her, wonder who she was and why she behaves like this. But, the truth of the truth is, this kind of behavior goes on all the time.

Think about the internet and all the cowards that hide behind screen names, they say all kinds of hurt-filled garbage and do not even care. Then, there are people like this lady—someone locked into the righteousness of their actions and their all-knowingness about the reality of everyone else.

I mean, when you look at the people who behave in this manner, it always seems they are the ones who are unhappy with their life and their life circumstance. Like the people who drive those really junky cars down the street and cut you off. As they take no pride in their life all they hold is bitterness and resentment. Do they care of if their car gets damaged? Of course not.

It's like when riots break out and people destroy their own neighborhood. They live in squalor, they have nothing, so they care about nothing. Thus, they want to hurt those who do have something. They want what is owned by that someone else, so they steal, ravage, and then destroy.

I have always warned my martial arts student to study the eyes of any person they are about to get into a physical confrontation with. There are some people who just do not care. And, if they do not care about themselves, they do not care what they will do to you. They are the ones you have to be very careful of, because fighting a person like that can be deadly.

It's like here in L.A., and in other places, as well, the homeless population has skyrocketed. Almost everyday, on the local news, you hear about some homeless individual viciously attacking, and in some cases killing, an unsuspecting stranger. It's really sad. But, these people have nothing to lose. In many cases they suffer from mental illness and refuse to take or cannot obtain the medication that would help their condition. Plus, law enforcement cannot enforce the law anymore, and the D.A's just cut the criminals free awaiting trial. So, they go out and do it again. The system is broken!

I think we've probably all encountered people like that woman who wanted to tell me about my life and felt she had the right to do so. I know this is not the first time something like this has happened to me. What can we do?

The answer is we must always be the bigger person. We must always be the better person. Now, this does not mean that our positive behavior is going to change that other individual in any manner or the way they treat other people. But, at least it will not escalate the situation, as that is what many of these people, who live on that low level of human consciousness, actually hope for. In fact, if you can, say something nice to them. Change the direction of what they have instigated by their unwanted, unwarranted statement.

The moral of this story is: today, if you are going to say anything at all, say something nice. Nice, always makes things better. And, if you believe you have the right to inflict your opinion about anybody's anything onto anyone else, think again. Because if what you are saying is not making something better, in the life of the person you are taking about, or to the entire world as a whole, really, wouldn't it just be better if you ate your words and kept them to yourself? Then, at least, you would not have added any agitation to an already turbulent world.

If you are not going to say something nice and positive, be wise enough not to speak.

The Silence of the Sound
19/Oct/2022 08:59 AM

  Having come of age in an era when the quality of sound was everything, I have long focused my life around the eminence of the sound(s) that I hear. For those of us who can remember, or for those of you who can't, if you look back to the movies of the era you will see that people personally owned things like reel-to-reel players, the speakers were always large, and people really worked to get the sound of the music they played on their home systems as good as it could possibly be. A great movie to watch to witness this is Boogie Nights; especially where Don Cheadle's character is selling stereo systems and hopes to, and eventually does, own his own stereo shop. People really cared about the quality of their sound.

  From the standpoint of a musician, this was also true. We all did, (and I think people still do in this arena of life), work to get that perfect sound out of their guitar and other instruments. As a young man, I would save up to buy this guitar, that amp, or a specific effect pedal, that I just knew would provide me with that quality of sound I was trying to obtain. My friends and I would spend hours discussing the realities of sound and how to get the characteristic and excellence of the tones we desired.

  Certainly, times have changed, and with that the minds of the masses have transformed. Digital altered everything. And yes, everything became so much easier to record and alter with that addition to our lives. But, I think back to the days when I owned one of the first prosumer, 4-Track reel-to-reel decks. I was so happy as I was finally able to record multiple tracks. I remember sitting for hours-upon-hours, sometimes days-upon-days, working to get a song laid down just right. Now, what took me days can happen in a few minutes. But, is the sound the same? No.

Then came the 4-Track cassette deck. I bought one of the first ones available in Tokyo, before they ever made it to the States. It was great! Recording on it became so much easier. Sadly, or maybe stupidly, I loaned it to a friend of mine who killed it. Sad, I really loved that deck. I wish I still had it today.

Yesterday, I was listing to the radio, as I was driving, and they played a song that the band had recorded on a vintage cassette deck. The sound was a bit gritty, but it really took me back to an era when you actually heard what you were listening to. A time when you (we all) actually listened for the subtleties of the sound.

I know a lot of musicians still hope to record on tape but now that has become very expensive. Well, high-functioning recording studios always have been expensive. But now, with so many people recording on their computer in their bedroom... ...I don't know, times have changed...

FYI: As I was speaking about RB7 yesterday... All the music for that was recorded on tape as was the music for *Samurai Vampire Bikers from Hell, Samurai Ballet,* and all my early Zen Films. If you truly listen, yes, there is a difference.

So, what is the point of all this blibber-blabber? It's about you and how you encounter your life. When you listen to a song do you truly listen to it or do you just love or hate it and/or tap your feet to the beat? Really, how do you encounter your life. Do you allow it to be just a thoughtless passing presentation, taking what is given to you, but never studying any of the subtleties? Or, do you delve deeply in the sounds that you hear, the things that you see, the people that you meet, the air that you breathe, and all that you are given the opportunity to feel through your sensory perception?

You can live your life in oblivion. Most people do. Or, you can make it a true experiential experience.

How are you going to live today? What are actually going to hear? Your choice.

Roller Blade Seven, Again
18/Oct/2022 12:36 PM

As I say far too often, *"A week rarely goes by where I am not asked some question about The Roller Blade Seven."* I was contacted on Facebook by a man who is apparently doing a podcast about RB7, and he asked me the question, *"How did you decide to mix roller blading and religion?"* So you can all know the answer to that question, if you ever questioned it at all, here's my response.

Hi Alexander,

It's essential to note that Don Jackson came up with the term Roller Blade before the skates were ever marketed. Roller equaling Skates and Blade equaling the Samurai Sword. Thus, *Roller Blade Seven* has nothing to do with rollerblade skates. Even though many people put the words Roller and Blade together when discussing or marketing the film, this is incorrect.

In terms of the, *"Religion,"* you ask about in RB7, Don did and I do base my entire life upon the various realms of spirituality, so it was only a natural progression for us to introduce that into the film. Plus, since the moment Don read my books: *Essence: The Zen of Everything* and *Zen O'clock: Time to Be,* he wanted to use the aphorisms presented in those books as the primary source of dialogue for the film. His idea, not mine. As spirituality is the basis of those books, the words presented in them helped to shape the direction of the film. From these factors, spirituality became a central focus of RB7 and its sequel *Return of the Roller Blade Seven.*

Hope this helps! If you have any other questions, feel free to ask, I will try to answer them.

All the best,
S.

      Also, somebody sent me a photo of a life-sized, art-piece cut out of Hawk (Me in RB7 Character) on Instagram the other day. The guy holding it was riding a skateboard. As I guess he didn't follow me, (or something???) I saw it in the message request section of my account and once I looked at it the photo seemed to disappear. I don't know, maybe I did something wrong??? So, if you know who that is or what that's about, hook me up and send me the photo again. I'll post it.

Who is Saying What and Why?
17/Oct/2022 02:17 PM

"Who is saying what and why?" Though this certainly is not an original aphorism, or anything like that. But, I believe this is an important question you must ask yourself as you percolate any words that are presented to you.

There has been a lot of talk about talk of late. Terms like, *"Fake news,"* and other descriptive jargon radiates throughout our everywhere. Though some of these expressionery phrases are interesting and even fun to use and/or to make fun of, they really tell us a lot about human culture.

Think about a time you heard something and you instantly believed it but it turned out to be false once you truly examined the claims. Think about a time when you believe something that someone told you and it turned out to be a fabrication of the truth or just a flat out lie. Think about a time when you read or heard something, you believed it, you spread those words to other people, but it turned out to not be the truth. Didn't that make you a liar?

How do you feel about that? How do you feel about the person where you heard the words from in the first place? And, do you ever contemplate any of this?

I think back to a time when someone was discussing Hitler and I was surprised to hear that they did not know the man was born in Austria. I explained that to them and thought nothing more about the conversation. A bit farther down the line, I heard someone making fun of this person as they were telling people that Hitler was born in Australia. Somehow, in their mind, I said Austria, but they translated that into Australia. They heard wrong, but they believed they were spreading some foundational knowledge to other people. Funny, yes. But, think how often this kind of stuff goes on all the time.

Though that is an exaggerated example, ask yourself, how often do you believe someone simply because they say something? Then, how often do you spread that knowledge, as false as it may be, to others? What about if what you were told was not the truth? Who have you hurt by speaking those words based in falsehood?

What I am saying here is that you really have be careful about who you believe. Though they may claim all kinds of foundational knowledge, you need to ask yourself, *"Who is saying what and why?"*

When most people speak, they possess a motive for saying what they are saying. If they are talking about some, *"Out there,"* knowledge or are speaking about someone else, you really need to question what is their motivation for communicating about anything at all: what is their true basis of knowledge, and is what they saying based upon a predetermined perspective and/or words being used to shift the thoughts of other people to their way of thinking?

Always listen but be careful what you believe.

Think about it.

She Gave Away My Good Luck
16/Oct/2022 02:48 AM

When I was in Bangkok, a week or so ago, I picked up this painting. The gallery owner, after packaging it for me, handed me this little elephant key chain trinket type of thing. She said, *"Thank you,"* and, *"This will bring you good luck."* Okay... Now, I've never been one of those people that was into that type of talisman stuff, but I appreciated the gesture. I didn't think too much about it.

Back home, my lady was collecting the gifts to give to her sister and her sister's kids today, and I guess she decided to throw that keychain into the pot. I didn't know about it until after it was done. But, in asking, it was gone. Did she give away my good luck?

Late into the late night of tonight, I was awoken from my sleep from this noise going on outside. It was a fight between two guys, and two girls, I guess??? I could hear the fists hitting the skin and one of the girls screaming. Neighbors were yelling, *"Go home, assholes!"* But, no cops came onto the scene. It seems the street and street activities always haunt and find me, even though I have long run away from them. Plus, I live in a very, (for lack of a better term), relatively exclusive community. Yet, there it was...

Earlier today, someone told me of some on-line rant that was going on about me, my filmmaking process, and my films. I never pay attention to that kind of stuff. Like I, and most other actual filmmakers say to the critics, *"What movies have you made?"* But, before I dozed off on the couch tonight, as I often tend to do, I pulled up a couple of my films on YouTube, just to give them a moment or two of a viewing. And yeah, they are okay. Thirty years deep and they are still a-okay. I suppose the critics still talking about movies I made on a zero budget twenty or thirty years ago and incorrectly describing my mindset, process, and technique of filmmaking is somehow casting me to infamy.

I guess I could say, *"Thank you."* But mostly, I think, *"Fuck you! Why don't you try getting it right."* Anyway…

So, this all fades into life. The life of the happening. I remember growing up in the ghetto, there was crime, fighting, and violence around me all the time. I remember living in Hollywood, when the sounds of the street and the police helicopters would wake me up most nights of the week. I hated that noise! Now, all these decades later, I still hear the punch in the face and the girl screaming about her boyfriend and people who have never made a film talking shit about my movies. I don't know??? Did my lady give my good luck away today or is this just the reality of the reality? …A world where people have nothing better to do than becoming lost in what they are feeling, leading to a punch in the face, talking shit about a craft that they have no concept about how to actually create, and waking up a neighborhood simply because they have nothing better to do than to scream about relationships and feelings that matter to one else but the people screaming?

I guess I need to go back to Bangkok. I'm always happier there anyway. I guess I need to go and pickup another painting and maybe the seller will give me another elephant keychain that promises good luck.

Never Ask for a Favor
15/Oct/2022 07:04 AM

Have you ever noticed that some people ask for a lot of favors? They ask you to do something and it seems so innocent but then it leads you down a road to a lot of problems?

Have you ever said, *"No,"* to one of these favor askers and then they got all incensed? Or, have you ever asked them for a favor, after you've done them a solid, and all they have is all of these excuses of why they just cannot help you out?

For me, whenever I ask anybody for anything, I always make sure that there is an element of give-back—that they are going to get something out of their effort in return for their doing. Then, though yes, they may be helping me out, they also will reap some benefit from their giving.

Whenever someone who has helped me out asks me for something, I always respond with a yes. They helped me, so I feel I must help them. But, I guess this is where all the problems of favor giving is formed.

Have you ever had somebody do something for you and it just kind of feels that they are doing it so they can get something out of you in the near future? Maybe they go all-in in doing the favor you asked of them—they do it one hundred percent, but then, almost immediately, they turn it around and they ask something BIG from you—something that really messes with your life space to do?

If you hadn't asked them, they probably wouldn't have asked you. So, who actually set the ball into motion?

Favors are a complicated thing. That's why I virtually never ask anything from anybody. It just walks everyone down a road where life gets so complicated.

So, next time you ask someone for some sort of help, think about what it is going to cost you a bit further down the line. Ponder what you are going to owe them. Question, what you asking, and them giving, will cause you to owe. Because if you ask and they give but then if they ask and you don't give, who's lap is that karma going to fall into?

From Behind
14/Oct/2022 07:23 AM

    I love photography that shows the landscape and the people of a specific region of a particular county. I've been taking photographs like that ever since I got my first reasonably good camera when I was thirteen, in 9th grade. I just love the way you can study those photographs for the nuisances and maybe really learn something while you are looking for the hidden elements.

    I follow some active photographers and some of the groups that post photographs from specific regions of the world on Facebook. I really don't want to know about people going to conventions and seeing some actor from times gone past or people trying to finance their horror film. (I don't like horror). Or, people soliciting a seminar they are going hold with some great grandmaster. And, all the stuff like that. But, to see a really interesting photograph, now that can be inspirational.

    Recently, there is something I've been noticing. I guess it's something that I've always known, but it is one of those things that you know but you don't bring that known knowledge to the forefront of your mind. I was taking note of the fact that a lot of the photographs I have been viewing, along with the city or country scape, show the back of a person or persons. Meaning, they were shot from behind that individual. I'm guess that is just something that happens naturally because you don't want to be rude and stick a camera in someone's face. I know I have followed this pattern, as well. Though, I suppose, with the advent of phone photography, grabbing concealed photographs anywhere/anytime has become so much more easy.

    I think back to the days when I used to carry three camera bodies with three different primary lenses with me wherever I went when I was out somewhere across the globe. That was a heavy bag to carry! Now, though I do always carry a camera, they are so much smaller and so much lighter, and, in reality, the iPhone can get just as good of a shot as I used to hope to get, but often never did, in those times, with all those cameras, all those years ago.

Back then, as now, unless someone is a willing participant, I really hate to just take their photograph. Don't you hate it when someone takes a photograph of you without your permission?

Thus, and therefore, I guess a lot of people follow this rule and a lot of photographs are taken from behind. Like I said, I know I have done this, as well. I think to some of my album or book covers and the central image is that of a person from behind.

I guess, at least in part, I got to thinking about this a week or so ago, when the people that handle the Swami Satchidananda account on Instagram posted a photo, from the early 1970s, where you can see the back of head sitting just to the right of my teacher. I know it was me. I remember the talk he gave that day very well. But, if you didn't know I was there and/or you didn't know what the back of my head looked like, you would never know it was me.

Contemplating all this, this AM, first I thought how something is lost in this process, as you don't get to see the face. And, a face is so illustrative. Some faces really pull you in. But then, thinking about it a little more, I realized that from behind there is so much more illusion, as so much is left to the imagination.

I think to the photographs I have taken and have used, where the rear of a person is central to the frame. …Of the one's I have used or have really liked, they were all chosen for a reason. They, like any good photograph, provides that level that causes the mind to study the photograph and to try to find all that is hidden within it.

So, in closing, faces are great. You can really learn a lot from studying a face. But, from behind, your mind is left to the realms of guessing, imagination, and the questioning of illusion. In some ways, isn't that just a more profound way to study life?

    Remember, there is wisdom in the unseen.

What You Say Matters
13/Oct/2022 08:48 AM

Currently, here in L.A., there is a big controversy going on with three City Council Members over a leaked audio tape where one of them made some very racial insensitive comments about another City Council Member's son and about some of the immigrant populations that inhabits certain sections of Los Angeles. There are all these protests going on for them to leave their seats. Even President Biden feels they should step down. The one actually making the comments did. The other two have not, at least not as of yet, but they will probably be forced to do so. The thing is, these comments were made a year ago. Throughout this time, they have kept their jobs, been paid by the taxpayers for doing their jobs, and if this tape was not leaked no one would have ever known how this woman, making the comments, truly felt. The other two at least did not appear to voice the same opinion(s), but they chuckled along to what she was saying.

Here's the thing, times have changed, you just cannot say, or maybe better put, even think, anything that is not positive, good, and caring anymore. Some may not like this fact, but that is the fact of the fact. Life has evolved and we must all evolve with this change. Really, think about it, isn't being positive and not saying negative things about someone/anyone better?

I think back to times gone past, it was very common to unleash racial slurs, to criticize anyone who you did not agree with, and label them this derogatory name or that. The world, at least certain sectors of the world, has changed. And, that is good thing.

I always hear about that the internet is filled with hate and hateful language, and I guess that is true. I just don't frequent those places, so I don't read it. How about you? How much negativity and/or hate/and/or hurt have you unleashed on the internet or in life? This is really a critical question you must ask yourself, because the fact of the fact is, you are either part of the evolution of making things better or you are part of the problem. Which one are you?

Though two of the members of that City Council conversation did not voice the level of negativity as this one woman did, they were there in that conversation, and they said nothing. They should have interceded. They should have stopped her negative rant. If one or both of these other two City Council Members would have stopped this woman's tirade, they would have been applauded.

I get it, sometimes mob mentality rules. People wish to support their superior or those they admire. But, hurt is hurt. Wrong is wrong. And, if all you do is chuckle while someone is voicing hate or hurt you are as much a part of the problem as they are.

I understand when some people rise to a position of power they feel all-empowered and they believe they can say or do whatever it is they want. Is that right? Is that good? Is that helpful? Or, is that just ego? If you or your words hurt anyone else, you have done nothing but hurt. And, hurt never helps. In others words, don't allow your lower self to control you.

I am sure there is no one out there who has not said some negative something about someone or something at some point in their life. But, that does not have to be the definition of who you are. If you hurt, you hurt, and hurt is never good, no matter who hears it. You need to be part of this evolution. Be the betterment. Never be part of the hurt.

* * *
12/Oct/2022 05:09 PM

Everybody does what they do on purpose, some people just live in denial of this fact; to themselves and to others.

When You've Blown It
11/Oct/2022 04:26 PM

Easy Rider is certainly one of the greatest movies ever made. It is a cinematic masterpiece. Near the end of the film there is that great moment when Peter Fonda's character looks at Dennis Hopper's character and says, *"We blew it."* Realizing that they had the chance to live something great and maybe even achieve some greater good, reach some higher goal, but they did not. I believe in everyone's life there is that moment when we each realize that we blew it. We should have taken one road, but, instead, we took what we realized was the wrong one. We should've veered left, but we turned right. We should have embraced a relationship with this person, but we did not. We shouldn't have been in a relationship with that person, but were. I'm sure some of my old girlfriends feel that way about me. And, the list goes on. In any case, we believe that we made the wrong decision. Sometimes these realizations happen right away, other times they occur years down the line. But, I do not believe that any of us is not left with the thought that we blew it at some point in our life.

Some people are very good about living in denial. They fill their time with work, family, fun, and/or whatever else it is that takes their mind off of their own truth. Others, believe that it all happened for a reason. But, did it? Is that a universal truth spouted from the mouth of some grand sage or is that just another form of denial?

Others just don't care. They especially don't care if the wrong turn they made hurt someone else. But, that is just selfishness and hurtful, delusional behavior. There is nothing right in that mindset.

No matter how hard we all try to fight it, in life we are going to make mistakes and we are going to realize that we blew it. Then what? What are you going to do to rechart that life event or to fix that mistake?

The fact is, we can never go back. We can never relive any life moment. Yes, we can chase after it. We can try to redo it. We can track down some person and try to undo what was done. But, what was done then, was done. A decision was made and that is that. Now, what?

It's essential to realize that what was offered to us once, most likely will never come our way again. Good or bad, that's the fact. Even if we are in some way able to recreate a moment or rekindle a relationship, what was then is not what is now. Again, now what?

Some people spend their entire life living in a state of regret, thinking about that wrong choice that they made. Most are not like that, however. That is not to say that most of us do not periodically ponder the what should have been/the what could have been, if only… But, all we are left with is what we are left with.

Take a moment, think about that time that you, *"Blew it."* What choice did you make? Why did you make that choice? And why, after the fact, did you realize it was the wrong choice to have made? Really think it through.

Imagining what would have been, *"If only,"* is just a fantasy, as you can never really know. So, don't get lost in that. But, what about now? What about where you find yourself in life at this moment? What can you do to live this moment to the best of your ability? What can you do right here, right now to make your today and your tomorrow better so that you will not feel like you blew it and maybe even take away some of the regret from that time when you feel that you made that wrong choice?

Think it through. Do something Right. Do something Positive. Make a Good Choice that will be regret free.

The Things You're Not Supposed to Be
11/Oct/2022 09:29 AM

I've been spending time in Bangkok again. I guess it was the pandemic and life and all that but it had been a few years since I was there. Once upon a time, in the long ago and the far-far away, I was there all the time. I lived there. I even had an apartment there for a time. Like I say in the intro to my book, Bangkok and the Nights of Drunken Stupor, *"To Manita S. and all her lies, Pichitra D. and her white powder truths, and mostly to the Goddess who has permeated my soul and left me with Siam vision."* Yeah, I'm always very happy there. Sadly, those people I reference in that intro are all gone now—as are most of my friends from the B'Kok of the '80s and the '90s. AIDS killed a lot, drugs the others, and some, (I guess), just old age and time to leave this place we call life. But, I was close to them. I really miss them. A few in particular.

Anyway, I had this weird flash of memory. I was staying at the legendary hotel, then known as, The Oriental. I was in my late twenties. I had been awarded my Ph.D. degree in 1987, when I was twenty-eight, and I was walking that path at that point in my life, so I used Doctor instead of Mister in my sign-ins. Now, I see all that as a bunch of unnecessary ego. But, back then… Anyway, the Thais have never been known for being subtle. I was having lunch at this one restaurant at the hotel one day and I could hear this one restaurant worker just going off on me, about me being a, *"Doctor."* He was talking about how I was too young, (I'm told I look young for my age—especially back then), about how I had long hair, and how I couldn't be a doctor and all that. The thing was, he was speaking in Thai so I'm sure he assumed I wouldn't understand him. Wrong. When he came to my table with some water, all nicey-nice, I asked, *"Why can't I be a doctor? I have a Ph.D. degree."* After that, and for the remainder of my stay, whenever I saw him, we were best buds. But, here's the thing, people think they know the what's-what about everything and everybody else. But, how can they? How can anybody truly know anything about anybody else, if you don't truly know them? Even then, you may be wrong.

It's like I got deeply involved in the martial arts and yoga very young in my life. Especially in the yoga and eastern spiritual circles, my friends would make jokes about how I was still just a teenager. From this, I became an instructor very early on. Back then, and even much later in my life, people have thrown shade about my credibilities. Especially in the martial arts, that kind of BS goes on all the time, but in spirituality, it should not exist. Well, it shouldn't exist in the martial arts either, but it has just become so common there, I guess it is somewhat expected. Not right, but predictable.

A funny story… I had my first studio when I was twenty-one. I thought people wouldn't want to study from someone so young, so if they asked, I lied and told them I was twenty-seven. But now, I am way deep in my life. Yet, and still, people want to cast judgements about who should be what and why they should or shouldn't be this or that. But, who are they that is casting that judgement? What all-powerful, all-knowing knowledge do they possess? It seems that all the one's casting the judgement ever are is the one's who have achieved the least. Like I always say, *"If you are thinking and speaking about someone else, that means that you are the one who is not worthy of talking about."*

Anyway, I'm bouncing back and forth between Bangkok again. It feels like such a blessing! Like Tokyo and Hong Kong, as the pandemic wains, (well I don't know about HK, the Powers That Be of the PRC have really fucked that place up), but I hope I can re-get my fix. I have deeply miss my time in those places.

Side story here: Coming home to L.A., a week or so ago, I got stuck in the airport lounge in Manila for like fourteen hours. Super Typhoon Karding hit and was passing overhead. You could see the intensity of the wind and the rain through the windows. I don't know why the airlines tried to fly that direction in the first place. But me, what do I know? Anyway, I eventually flew home via an insanely bumpy fourteen hours flight.

But, back to the point… Who knows what and why? Why do you think you know whatever it is you think you know about someone else? And, most importantly, what if you're wrong?

Walking On a Road to Nowhere
06/Oct/2022 08:35 AM

I think if we look to the current situation with North Korea, and how they just launched a ballistic missile across Japan, we can question, why are they behaving in that manner? Their people are starving, they are a lone wolf trying to prove some point that no one else even understands, yet they continue to walk down a road to nowhere. If they would just stop, if they would simply open up, they could become a part of the world community, and their people could flourish.

Their behavior is nothing new. It has been going on since the end of the Korean War. But, when something is not working, why do some people refuse to change the path they are on?

I think if we look to the people we know or have known in our own lives, we can see this same pattern of behavior. Some people simply take to a road and they refuse to leave it, no matter how much their life, based upon that chosen road, is not working. We can ask, why? But, some people will simply not change.

I think to people I have interacted with. …Some people who spend years attempting to enter the film industry, I provided them with a pathway, but due to their own inner-developed demons, (for lack of a better term), they sabotage the relationship. Thus, they are left with nothing more than the ever-remaining desire to make movies. But, if they had followed the path of others that I, (and other people), had opened the door for, they could have lived the life they hoped for.

This is the same with people I have known in the world of the music business, (via its expansive nature). Some I have known, I believe, should have become successful. But, they did not. Then, they were left fighting for money for the rest of their life. Did they change? No. Yet, they could have. I even suggested some very concrete methods for this one music business owner to get back on his feet financially. But, he was stubborn. He didn't even try. At one point, a guitar collector friend he had passed away and left him his entire collection to liquify and pay off his debt to this one woman who had loaded him a large amount of money. The guy sold most of the collection and kept a large part of that money for himself, however, not paying off all of the debt. That's just not right. What kind of a friend is that? And, here's the thing, we all need money to survive, but if what you are doing to get that money involves you stealing from someone else, shouldn't you reconsider the road you are on?

Like I joking say, *"If you can't swim, don't dive into the ocean."* But, this is what people do. Then, even though they can't swim, they keep trying to survive—they keep treading water, trying to keep from drowning. But, is that how life should be lived in a constant state of struggle? I don't think so.

There's the thing, we all want what we want. We all have a dream. We all want to live our life they way we wish to live it. We all want to do things the way we want to do them. But, if it ain't workin,' it ain't workin.' If you want to live a life of peace, embracing a greater and a better wholeness, you need to be willing to adapt and change. Sure, maybe you will not be living on the grand scale you hoped to achieve, but is your living in chaos a better alternative? Probably not. Be willing to change the road you are walking upon and your life may become a whole lot better. Think about it…

Coffee at Two
05/Oct/2022 02:08 PM

Back in the days when Starbucks was relatively new to the L.A. area, more than twenty years deep now, I used to go to one of the nearby Starbucks. This was long before there was one on every corner. I used to plan my day that I would head out around two or so in the afternoon in order to get there by 2:30. I would grab a latte, nonfat, of course, and maybe one of their tasty gingerbread man cookies they had back in the day. I would kick back and ponder life, reality, and the day. It wasn't that it was even that great of a location. It wasn't even that close to where I lived. It wasn't like it had a nicely shaded patio surrounded by pant, flowers, or tree, or anything. It was just a place with tables that were next to the roadways that ran through this shopping plaza that housed, predominately, a Home Depot. Looking back, I really don't know why, but that is just the thing I did.

I got to be friends with the baristas at that location. The fact was, it was rare that I would ever pay for my drink. They always just hooked me up and refused to take my money. I always found that to be such a nice gesture. I remember, a few years later, when I moved from the beach to a location overlooking the ocean and began going to another Starbucks, (most of the time), it was always a shock that nobody hooked me up anymore. I had to pay.

Those two Starbuck's location were probably only a mile or so apart. But, the whole vibe was so different, even though this new/my new location had much better patio seating.

Every now and then, like today, my almost daily journey to that Starbucks comes to mind. On one hand, I question, why? Why did I go there? What did I find? On the other hand, I wish I had the motivation to do that again, on a more or less daily basis. But, I don't.

Now, I grab my daily dose of Starbucks, usually in the AM, at a location overlooking the ocean, on my way to wherever it is I am going. I rarely stop and sit there, however, as it is generally far too crowded. Now, everyone seems to honker down. They have their laptop and are doing business or writing the next great screenplay or novel. You can expect them to be there for hours. ...I know when I pull up, if there is a seat, they are there. And, they have not moved an inch when I leave.

Moments of pondering life... Moments of agitated silence are really important for life, I believe. It is a true meditation. A place to just sit and be. Alone, but not alone. Because inside there is very little illusion to be found. But outside, you never know what you will find.

Anyway... No great philosophic revelation here. Just a remembrance of a time gone past. I am sure, you, like I, have those moments, those things you used to do but do no longer. Like I, maybe you don't remember why it changed either. But, it did. And, it seems even though we try sometimes, we just can never go back.

I wonder what all of those barista friends of mine are up to now??? It's been a long-long time. I hope their life turned out okay.

Artistic Intent
05/Oct/2022 06:24 AM

    I was kicking around this art complex in Bangkok about a week ago. I walked into one of the galleries and there was this girl, who I realized was the artist, standing in the center of the room having a man creating a video of her moving in association with her art works. Nothing vastly new in that. But, it did set me to thinking about the intent of the artist.

    Once upon a time, in the long ago and the far-far away, back in the '80s, when this building was constructed, and well into the '90s, this structure used to be home to a number of boutique style shops. It was always a very nice, well-maintained space. Somewhere along the way they decided to turn it into a gallery space. They also moved several of the high-end Thai antique shops that used to be over on Rama IV Road inside the structure. With the massive revamping of Bangkok, over the past twenty years, bringing in a lot of truly specular skyscrapers, much of the old vibe of Bangkok is long gone. Anyway…

    Here was this girl, inside this gallery, posing for the camera, and having her paintings exhibited.

    I believe this space was a pay to play scenario. I'm sure the gallery owners pick and choose who they allow to pay to play but the way most the galleries in this space are set up as single artist shows, it just lends itself to the obvious of the obvious.

    Certainly, there is nothing wrong in paying to play. This kind of stuff goes on all over the place all the time. An artist, by how ever you define that term, wants the world to find out about them, so they do what they must do to get their vision out there.

    This is where I believe the essence of art comes into play. An artist creates. End of story. They inhabit a creative vision, and they create it. That's what makes them an artist.

In that and of that there is a truth, a purity, and an all-encompassing wholeness. They create. This is something that much of the world does not do.

Now, this is not to say the artist is somehow superior. It is simply stating that they do what others do not.

Enter the critic. The other component in this equation. Like I stated just yesterday in this blog, and I have been saying for years, *"If you do not have your own unique creative vision, you criticize the unique vision that others possess."* Meaning, there is a whole plethora of people out there throwing shade on the creative works of others, yet they are not the ones on the front lines actually creating something new, unique, and artistic. Like the old saying goes, *"Everyone is a critic."* In fact, think how many people are out there on the internet actually making a living by systematically critiquing the creative works of other people. On even a more diabolical level, think about all the people who just insult the creative works of the artist simply because they can: anywhere/anyplace.

Now, as an artist, I, of course, do not appreciate this. I see the lack of vision or understanding in these people who spend their time living in a state of negativity and hate, when they could be living in a space of creativity. It's all a choice, you know. Who gives them the right to do this? Answer: You do. If you support negativity on any level, you are part of the problem, not part of the cure. Think about it…

As I watched this girl, doing what she was doing, and as I studied her art, I realized I was not a super fan of what she had created but that did not make me descend to a lower level and unleash criticism. What she was doing was actualizing her vision of art as she saw it. She was creating. She was a creative. That in and of itself should be celebrated, never diminished.

I think this is an important thing to think about as you pass through life. What do you like and why do you like it? What do you do with your likes and your dislikes? Do you allow your likes and your dislikes to spur your conversation? Do you allow your likes and your dislikes to cause you to unleash your opinion possibly hurting the life of the artist who is actually out there creating something—attempting to make the world a more artist environment?

Mostly, what art are you creating? If you're not creating art, but you are creating criticism, how do you believe that makes anything in this world any better?

Be more than your opinion, because what does you opinion actually add to the betterment of the world? Create, and from your creation, a whole new world of artistic joy may be given birth to.

* * *

04/Oct/2022 02:26 PM

If you do not have your own unique creative vision, you criticize the unique vision that others possess.

* * *
04/Oct/2022 10:14 AM

Who's going to cry when you die?

* * *

04/Oct/2022 10:08 AM

If you didn't do it in the first place you wouldn't have to try to undo it.

The Books That Nobody Reads
03/Oct/2022 08:51 AM

A couple of months ago I was able to pick up a very rare hardcover copy of the spiritual classic, *Be Here Now* by Baba Ram Dass. Certainly, for anyone who grew up in the era that I did, and was drawn to spirituality, this was one of the must-read texts. It really set a standard for an entire community.

The copy I found for sale on-line had spent much of its life in the library of a local community college here in the Los Angeles area. So, one would think, particularly back in the 1970s, that a lot of people would have checked out and read this library copy. What I found truly interesting, looking at the library card that they put in those library-based books, is that from 1973, when I guess it arrived at the library, until 1989 when, I guess, it moved away, only like ten people had checked it out. That's crazy! A spiritual classic like this and no one cared enough to read it.

I think this fact is very revealing. I mean it tells a story on so many levels.

Even though this book lived its life in L.A., a place where most would consider to be a liberal, free-thinking, place to dwell, very few cared to find the information this book provides. Even at the college level, where many are considered to be searching, seeking, and trying to find meaning in their life; nada, very few people checked it out.

But, look around you, look into your own mind, how much spirituality do you find? Are you seeking a deeper meaning to life? If you are, great! Good for you! But, most are not.

There is no right or wrong in this equation, it's just an illustration of life. A sad one, I believe. Not caring about spirituality means that, most likely, you do not possess a moral code. And, from this, this is where all of the problems of the world begin.

Now, I'm not being all judgey here or anything. I'm just stating a fact. How many people do you know, who are not spiritually based, that truly seek the betterment of all mankind? How many people who do not identify as being openly spiritual, do you know, that set about on a path of truly helping others? Few, I believe.

Since the dawn of the New Age, there have been those who have hated on Western-based, Eastern Spirituality. And, I get all that. But, if you step beyond judgement, good is good is good. It's a simple as that. And, no matter how you get to good is unimportant in the grand scheme of life. Those who do good are good. They intentionally help the greater whole. Whatever gets them there, to do that good, I think is great. But, and as is illustrated by the few people who checked out this copy of the book, few people even care enough to learn how to try.

There is no big point I am trying to make here. This is simply an observation about the reality of reality. But, I will say, if you cannot care about the greater good of the all, the everybody, and the everything—if you do not have a personal pathway to help those in need and to hurt no one, what does that say about you? If all you think about is you, how, on any level, can that be seen as good, whole, helping, and caring?

So today, let's all of us do something good. Let's get out there and remove any negativity we may encounter or we may have instigated. Whether you consider yourself walking the spiritual path or not, let's get out there and do something good. Let's get out there and help. Believe me, one small good deed can set a whole course of goodness in motion.

* * *
02/Oct/2022 05:06 AM

You're willing to talk but are you willing to listen?

Photographs of Memories Past
01/Oct/2022 06:48 AM

Over the past year or two, I've been uploading more and more of my feature films to YouTube. I've been on YouTube forever. But, in earlier times, a decade or more ago, I just put up film trailers and the like. Then, as time went along, I began to put up some of my shorts and full-length abstract pieces of cinema. Then/now, I began to put up some of my full-feature releases.

As I've discussed in the past, the times of indie cinema have just changed. Once upon a time, in the long ago and the far-far away, there was money to be made. But, with everyone becoming a filmmaker... ...Well, that is not really the case anymore. But, that's not the point in any of this...

In May of 2001, I was filming a movie. It was all going along pretty good. Two of the main components of the film, became what I would call, *"Friends."* One was a, *"Guy,"* the other was a, *"Girl."* The, *"Guy,"* was originally one of my students at U.C.L.A. Though a couple of years older than I, he was a talented actor who wanted to get into the actual filmmaking game, so he took one of my courses. The, *"Girl,"* also very talented, was young and new to L.A., and cast from the depth of the indie film casting newspaper, Dramalogue. She worked on the first film the, *"Guy,"* and I put together and I recognizing her talent so I called her back for round two on our next feature film.

All was going pretty well on this film. One night, after filming was completed, the two of us, and our cameraman, decided to go out to dinner. That's what this film, I am discussing, is based upon.

I handed the cameraman my Sony VX2000, one of the greatest indie film cameras ever made, (of that era), and told him, not to turn it off, no matter what. Of course, throughout the evening, I would periodically take over cameraman duties, and because of this, he also became a part of this little ditty and of the actual film we were making, as the footage shot was all so Zen.

Anyway, I got to thinking about this movie, a little while back, and pulled out the master. Watching it, I saw the magic that the three, (and to a lesser degree), four of us possessed in that moment. The Girl, the Guy, and I were close. We really clicked. You could see it in the footage. Were we in character? Of course, we were. But, in those characters, there was also an essence of pure realism. The affection was obvious.

As is the case with many of life's interactions, the three of us went our separate ways soon after that. The, *"Girl,"* I used in another film. Then, she went on to work in the A-market for a time. I was so happy for her! The, *"Guy,"* he went on to make his own movie. Good for him!

A voice mail was passed back and forth, every now and then for a time, but that was that. The last time I heard from the, *"Girl,"* was when her mother contacted me asking for a copy of the poster of the first film she did with me, as that was her first co-starring role. Though I never actually had any posters printed, I did have the poster designed and was happy to send them a copy of the design of it on disk. I told her mother when she printed it to hook me up with a copy, but I never heard from any of them, ever again. Oh well...

Where are they now? No idea??? It doesn't look like either of them ever took to social media, which I believe is a good thing. Gone... But, the memory locked into that movie is still alive.

As I watched it, I realized we lived those moments, over twenty-one years ago. Wow... That's a long time. I wondered what they look like now??? Me, I feel the same. Though I certainly was not what could be considered young back then. I don't know, maybe I was forty-two or forty-three. But then, as now, I feel so young. Physically, I think I look pretty much the same. Them, I have no idea about??? People can change a lot in twenty plus years...

But, think about this, and this is what I am thinking about... If that moment had not been filmed; sure the three/four of us may still remember it, but it would be lost to the hands of times, like so many other life-moments lived. Think about your life. Think about all the things you have done. Think about all of those happy moment when you were doing something with friends. Most likely you didn't film it. Maybe you took a few photos, now that taking photos has become so easy. But, a photo is not a true documentation of the expression of the lived reality. It is solely a captured and posed second of what really took place.

I don't know... I was going to put this movie up on YouTube... But, I think not. At least not right now... It's far too personal. Sure, it's already up on places like Amazon Prime Video, if you care to view it. It's been there for years. And, it's been out on DVD for well over a decade; almost two. But, nobody really cared/nobody really cares, even though it's a great example of *Cinéma vérité*. I noticed a review written about it several years deep now, and the reviewer just didn't get it. All he could do was throw hate. But, I get it, how could he understand it, it was not his life-moment lived.

Think about this, if you had footage filmed, and movies made, about all of those special times you have lived, think how much deeper your knowledge of Self would be and how much more understanding of how you used to be and how you used to feel could be experienced. If those moments were captured in time, wouldn't your life have somehow meant that something more?

* * *
30/Sep/2022 01:05 PM

If you get away with it, did you get away with it?

* * *
30/Sep/2022 01:05 PM

You can do whatever it is that you want to do but that doesn't mean that there won't be consequences.

Hardly Living on Yesterday
29/Sep/2022 07:23 AM

    What is new in your life right now? What is different in what you are doing today, compared to what you did yesterday? What new things have you learned? What new experiences have you undertaken?

    In the life of most people, they lock themselves into a mindset of the same. They do what they do until they can do it no longer. Most, look to their past experiences for what they will do today. Many listen to music from yesterday and remember the doings that were done in the past. How about you? How much of your today is based on today and how much of your today is based on yesterday?

    What did you do different this morning? Different, from what you did yesterday morning? What did you change? How did your life evolve?

    As you lived through your yesterday, what changed from the day before that and the day before that and the day before that?

    Your memories are based upon what you have done? How many new memories have you developed?

    Most people look to the doings of others for guidance in what they, themselves, will do today. They study what others have done. Decide if they like it. And, if they do, that is what they do. If they don't like what others have done, that is what they don't do. But, in all of that mimicking they have chartered no new territory, uniquely defined as their own. All they are doing is following a path developed for them by the creative mind of someone else.

    How about you? Where is your mind focused? Is it framed by what others have done? Or, is it a distinctive creation, created only by yourself?

    Life is a pathway of exploration. How much exploring are you doing, verses how much are you doing in the doing of what you have done before?

Today is a new day, experience it as such. Don't lock yourself into yesterday.

Friend or Foe
28/Sep/2022 04:33 PM

We all have our interpersonal relationships. With each of them, we must strike a balance as to what they bring to us, and we bring to them. None are perfect. Each has its ups and its downs. That's just life.

Through understanding that each relationship is not perfect, we choose to find and accept a balance of mutual acceptability and forgiveness. Yes, forgiveness, because as each relationship is not perfect, there is always a give and a take. We must accept the good with the bad.

But, there comes a point where we must decide if the bad overpowers the good—the doing of something that is not right, weights more heavily on our minds than the goodness we gain. Then, it may be time for us to leave that relationship behind.

I think back to this one friendship I had. It was a long-standing friendship, decades in the making. Though not perfect, as no relationship ever is, it filled a spot in my life, and I believe one in the life of that other person. What happened that lead to my stepping away was very slow in its making.

This relationship revolved around the world of music. And, I guess that's what brought it down.

My friend owned and operated a, *"Shop."* Long before the days of eBay, and other online services. When I wanted to move a guitar or something along, I would try selling it via his shop. I think to this one vintage bass I brought in for him to sell for me. No bid deal, though it was a very specific, unique piece of musical craftsmanship. I left it and a few months later I get a call that he had sold it for four hundred something dollars. Low, I thought, for the rarity of the piece, but what could I do? My friend took his twenty percent cut, and that was that. Jump forward a few weeks and my lady was doing what she was doing back then, having a monthly tea session with her mother, her sister, and her aunt. This time, it was to be held at our place. Not wanting to be around to interrupt any of the family fun they were to have, I headed out. While out, I popped into this one guitar shop up in West Hollywood that focused on vintage gear. In there, I saw the bass, my friend had sold for me. The price tag, over two-thousand dollars. Obviously, what his customer and so-called, *"Friend,"* had done was to buy the bass to resell it to this shop for a vast profit. Initially, I believe my friend knew the value of the bass and so I didn't argue the price he sold it for. But, he did not. Did he just take the money and run? Or, did he sell it for more and not tell me the true amount he got for the instrument? Though my friend denied and denied my claims, and that the bass I saw was not even my one-time bass, (though I knew that it was), that question always remained in the back in my mind.

Skip forward a number of years; my friend calls me up one day and tells me he knows someone who wants to buy this very rare guitar I owned for $8,000.00. I was at one of those points in my life where I was a bit cash poor, you know how that is, and I could use the money. So, I again agree, trusting that my friend knew what a fair price for the instrument was. He took his $2,000.00 commission and I got six G's. But, it was soon after this that I came to find out that the guitar was valued in the neighbor of $75,000.00 to 100,000.00, not $8,000.00. When I would periodically visit with my friend, I would bring up this fact. Again, he would deny that number. But, did he know and sell me short, not telling me the true amount he sold the guitar for, (as I knew he was in desperate need of money), or did he just sell it for a low-ball price before researching the true value of the instrument? In either case, just like with the bass, I got screwed. And, these weren't the only times this type of situation took place.

I continued to see him for the next few years. But, as time moved along, the loss of those instruments, at the hands of this man, and for far less money than I should have received, continued to haunt my feelings about our relationship. Was it my fault for letting him sell those instruments in the first place? Absolutely! Of course, it was. But, that's the thing about friendship, and that's what keeps them together or what breaks them apart; trust. Eventually, based on these factors, I just did not feel comfortable hanging out with him anymore.

These days, every now and then, I get a call from the guy: when something is going on, a mutual friend has died, or on my birthday. Me, I never respond. Though I wish him nothing but the best, his action lead to my not trusting him and regretting that I allowed him to sell my instruments. And, due to him leading me into those deals, and others, that were less than truly beneficial for me, I question, were we ever friends at all?

The thing is, most people don't possess the dedication and/or the fortitude to make things right, when they've done something that hurt someone else. They only think about themselves and maybe even make excuses or give themselves justification for what they have done. Thus, friendships are lost.

So, all of this is just something to think about as you pass down the road of life. Life is about relationships. All relationships are based upon how you treat the other person and how the other person treats you. Are you only in it for you? Are they only in it for themselves? And, no matter who is doing what, if you are self-motivated or unthinking in any of your actions regarding that other individual—if you hurt them, are you truly their friend at all?

* * *
27/Sep/2022 11:39 PM

If you don't know what a symbol means that symbol has no meaning to you.

Sitting in Your Own Peace
27/Sep/2022 03:26 AM

I was taking one of those long, fourteen-hour, transpacific flights. The plane left in the evening and was chasing the darkness across the globe. So, I guess, wherever it was we were flying, it was night. The window shades were pulled down, the cabin lights were off, and everyone in my cabin had their seats in full flat-out bed position and they were sleeping. It was about halfway through the flight, and I woke up thirsty, so I moved up to the crew section to request a water. As I pushed back the curtains, I notice a female crew member, sitting in her crew chair, in this small hallway that connected the two main aisles to each side of her. I glanced her direction and I immediately saw she was awake but was just sitting there with a wall just a few inches in front of her. She was awake. Her eyes were open. She was completely aware, but she was totally still. She sat there in a state of unmoving fully aware silence, meditatively staring at the wall in front of her. Aware but in a state of absolute peace. I was awe struck.

There is the meditative practice in Zen Buddhism known as Wall Gazing. It is sometimes referred to as, *"Bìguān."* In one of the legends it is told that the great sage Bodhidharma performed this practice for nine years before finding his ultimate pathway to the truth.

This meditation technique is one of the most basic, yet most useful forms of centering the mind and reaching a meditative state of consciousness, while not following the more traditional path of meditation where the eyes are close. It is performed by simply sitting in front of a wall, isolating a point on that wall, focusing on it, and allowing your mind to meditatively become silence. That focal point on the wall is where your consciousness is placed. Whenever your mind wanders, you bring your focus back to the place on that wall.

There she was, this stewardess. One would not generally think of a stewardess as a Zen Masters. But, in essence, why not? She was in the midst of doing her job, but she was in a state of meditative mindfulness. How profound is that?

I believe that few of us can achieve that level of peace while we are in the middle of doing our job. Most, are wrapped up in the game, whatever that game may be, and are thinking about The Doing.

As we all understand, very few people care about the true depth of meditation, on any level, all they think about is the Out There. But, contemplate this, if you can be so Self Aware that even in the midst of doing your job you can find that place of still and peace within yourself, how much more pure would your life become? How much clearer would your mind be in the realms of true reality? Yes, most are driven to Do in their job. They think about what they are doing, or they are thinking about anything else, but they are thinking, they are not, what I like to call, Peace Aware. From this, all life is lived defined by the churning movement of The Doing. But, in that Doing, no peace or enlightenment will ever be known.

I believe we can all find inspiration from this young stewardess; doing her job but able to sit in peace as it is being done.

Remember this story. Try it. Sit down in the chaos of whatever it is you are doing and embrace the silence, know the peace. From this, the divine grace of true meditation may be known and, you never know, you may find an entirely new way to encounter reality.

She looked up at me. I asked if I could have a water. She told me she would get it for me and bring it to my seat. A few moments later, she did.

I didn't have any way to verbalize my feelings towards her and how inspirational her meditative actions were. But, if nothing else, perhaps I can spread them out to you, where you may learn from them and possibly find a new and better way to encounter life. Wherever you find yourself, sit in your own peace.

Parking Lot Talk
17/Sep/2022 07:39 AM

Sadly, I had to go to a funeral yesterday. That's one of the sorrowful realities about life, the older you get, the more people you witness passing on.

The funeral was for my aunt in-law. The wife of my wife's mother's brother. Good lady. She was born in Japan occupied Korea. So, due to the brutal occupation of Japan, the conditions of her early life were not good. I think most people don't think about stuff like that anymore, Japan's occupation of places like Korea and Eastern China and all the devastation that they brought. Anyway, she was here, lived her life, had five sons, and now she is gone. It's never easy when someone you know passes on.

I think most Westerners don't know about this fact, but the Christian Church is really the lifeblood of modern Korean-American society. It is at the heart of their culture. One may question, why did this group of Asian peoples so heartily adopted a religion that was not their own, but that is an entirely different subject. Nonetheless, it is what truly runs, entirely, through their culture. As such, most Korean-Americans attend Sunday service.

Ever since I first became involved with the Korean-American community, as a young boy, via the martial arts, I would periodically interact with this Korean church going culture. It is a sight. Every Sunday, go to any Korean-American church and there is tons of people, true believers, in attendance. But, before I get too far off point…

As my aunt in-law was Korean, her Korean minister provided the service yesterday. As he was giving his eulogy, he brought up the fact that she never participated in, *"Parking Lot Talk."* I'd never heard that term before. But, he described it as what many in the congregation do after the service. They go out into the parking and complain about whatever, gossip, and the like. If you know anything about

Korean culture, this is a very common mindset. I just never heard it labeled before. But, the minister spoke of how she never did this. Instead, she worked to try to make things better.

"Parking Lot Talk," it made me think about how so many people base their life on this mindset. Particularity now, in this age of the internet, all a lot of people do is talk about nothing, complain, criticize, and gossip. But, how few step up to the plate and do something that truly makes the world a better place?

The minister spoke about how my aunt in-law would do things like help clean up the trash in the parking lot, help to put a tarp over a leaking roof on the church, and the like. Though some may consider these small things, if those things are not attended to, how will anything get better? If those things are not done, things will only get worse.

Life is only lived for a very short amount of time. It's here and then it's gone. It's always sad to witness those we know, those we care about, and those we like or respect, pass on. Me, I'm getting rather long in the tooth, as the old saying goes. Me too… I won't be around that much longer. How about you? Where do you find yourself on the stage of life? How about those you know and care about? Where are they in their life-scape? We're all only going to be here, in life, for a moment. Is all you're going to do based on Parking Lot Talk? Or, are you going to get out there and do something positive and make the world a better place?

That eulogy was an interesting place to gain a new realization. One I never saw coming. We all need to stop the Parking Lot Talk and get out there and pick up the trash.

RIP Wesungmo. Thanks for creating your sons who, two of them, helped me produce a couple of my books. Thanks for your and all of their friendships. Thanks for the holiday dinners. Thanks for being a part of the life play I lived! You are remembered. You will be missed.

THE ZEN

www.ingramcontent.com/pod-product-compliance
Lightning Source LLC
Chambersburg PA
CBHW070603170426
43201CB00033B/1674